RETHINKING GENESIS 1–11

The Didsbury Lectures
Series Preface

The Didsbury Lectures, delivered annually at Nazarene Theological College, Manchester, are now a well-established feature on the theological calendar in Britain. The lectures are planned primarily for the academic and church community in Manchester but through their publication have reached a global readership.

The name "Didsbury Lectures" was chosen for its double significance. Didsbury is the location of Nazarene Theological College, but it was also the location of Didsbury College (sometimes known as Didsbury Wesleyan College), established in 1842 for training Wesleyan Methodist ministers.

The Didsbury Lectures were inaugurated in 1979 by Professor F. F. Bruce. He was followed annually by highly regarded scholars who established the series' standard. All have been notable for making high calibre scholarship accessible to interested and informed listeners.

The lectures give a platform for leading thinkers within the historic Christian faith to address topics of current relevance. While each lecturer is given freedom in choice of topic, the series is intended to address topics that traditionally would fall into the category of "Divinity." Beyond that, the college does not set parameters. Didsbury lecturers, in turn, have relished the privilege of engaging in the dialogue between church and academy.

Most Didsbury lecturers have been well-known scholars in the United Kingdom. From the start, the college envisaged the series as a means by which it could contribute to theological discourse between the church and the academic community more widely in Britain and abroad. The publication is an important part of fulfilling that goal. It remains the hope and prayer of the College that each volume will have a lasting and positive impact on the life of the church, and in the service of the gospel of Christ.

1979	Professor F. F. Bruce†	*Men and Movements in the Primitive Church*
1980	The Revd Professor I. Howard Marshall	*Last Supper and Lord's Supper*
1981	The Revd Professor James Atkinson†	*Martin Luther: Prophet to the Church Catholic*
1982	The Very Revd Professor T. F. Torrance†	*The Mediation of Christ*
1983	The Revd Professor C. K. Barrett†	*Church, Ministry and Sacraments in the New Testament*
1984	The Revd Dr A. R. G. Deasley	*The Shape of Qumran Theology*
1985	Dr Donald P. Guthrie†	*The Relevance of John's Apocalypse*
1986	Professor A. F. Walls	The Nineteenth-Century Missionary Movement**

1987	The Revd Dr A. Skevington Wood†	*Reason and Revelation*
1988	The Revd Professor Morna D. Hooker	*Not Ashamed of the Gospel: New Testament Interpretations of the Death of Christ*
1989	The Revd Professor Ronald E. Clements	*Wisdom in Theology*
1990	The Revd Professor Colin E. Gunton†	*Christ and Creation*
1991	The Revd Professor J. D. G. Dunn	*Christian Liberty: A New Testament Perspective*
1992	The Revd Dr P. M. Bassett	*The Spanish Inquisition***
1993	Professor David J. A. Clines	*The Bible in the Modern World*
1994	The Revd Professor James B. Torrance†	*Worship, Community, and the Triune God of Grace*
1995	The Revd Dr R. T. France†	*Women in the Church's Ministry*
1996	Professor Richard Bauckham	*God Crucified: Monotheism and Christology in the New Testament*
1997	Professor H. G. M. Williamson	*Variations on a Theme: King, Messiah and Servant in the Book of Isaiah*
1998	Professor David Bebbington	*Holiness in Nineteenth Century England*
1999	Professor L. W. Hurtado	*At the Origins of Christian Worship*
2000	Professor Clark Pinnock†	*The Most Moved Mover: A Theology of God's Openness*
2001	Professor Robert .P Gordon	*Holy Land, Holy City: Sacred Geography and the Interpretation of the Bible*
2002	The Revd Dr Herbert McGonigle	John Wesley**
2003	Professor David F. Wright†	*What Has Infant Baptism Done to Baptism? An Enquiry at the End of Christendom*
2004	The Very Revd Dr Stephen S. Smalley	*Hope for Ever: The Christian View of Life and Death*
2005	The Rt Revd Professor N. T. Wright	*Surprised by Hope*
2006	Professor Alan P. F. Sell	*Nonconformist Theology in the Twentieth Century*
2007	Dr Elaine Storkey	Sin and Social Relations**
2008	Dr Kent E. Brower	*Living as God's Holy People: Holiness and Community in Paul*
2009	Professor Alan Torrance	Religion, Naturalism, and the Triune God: Confronting Scylla and Charybdis**
2010	Professor George Brooke	The Dead Sea Scrolls and Christians Today**
2011	Professor Nigel Biggar	*Between Kin and Cosmopolis: An Ethic of the Nation*
2012	Dr Thomas A. Noble	*Holy Trinity: Holy People: The Theology of Christian Perfecting*
2013	Professor Gordon Wenham	*Rethinking Genesis 1–11***
2014	Professor Frances Young	
2015	Professor Elaine Graham	

Rethinking Genesis 1–11

Gateway to the Bible

THE DIDSBURY LECTURES 2013

GORDON J. WENHAM

CASCADE Books • Eugene, Oregon

RETHINKING GENESIS 1–11
Gateway to the Bible

The Didsbury Lectures Series

Copyright © 2015 Gordon J. Wenham. All rights reserved. Except for brief quotations in critical publications or reviews, no part of this book may be reproduced in any manner without prior written permission from the publisher. Write: Permissions, Wipf and Stock Publishers, 199 W. 8th Ave., Suite 3, Eugene, OR 97401.

Cascade Books
A Division of Wipf and Stock Publishers
199 W. 8th Ave., Suite 3
Eugene, OR 97401

www.wipfandstock.com

Quotations from Stephanie Dalley's *Myths from Mesopotamia* used with permission from Oxford University Press. The Holy Bible, English Standard Version® (ESV®). Copyright © 2001 by Crossway, a publishing ministry of Good News Publishers. All rights reserved. ESV Text Edition: 2011.

ISBN 13: 978-1-4982-1742-2

Cataloging-in-Publication data:

Wenham, Gordon J.

The Didsbury Lectures Series

Rethinking Genesis 1–11 : gateway to the Bible / Gordon J. Wenham.

x + 76 p. ; 23 cm. Includes bibliographical references.

ISBN 13: 978-1-4982-1742-2

Genesis 1–11. 2. Bible—Theology. I. Series. II. Title.

B765 W46 2015

Manufactured in the U.S.A.

Contents

Preface | ix

1. Rethinking Genesis 1: A Creation Designed for Man | 1
2. Rethinking Genesis 2–4: Creation Disrupted by Man | 18
3. Rethinking Genesis 6–9: Creation Destroyed and Restored | 35
4. Rethinking Genesis 5–11: Creation in Need of Redemption | 52
5. Epilogue: The Hope of New Creation | 66

Bibliography | 75

Preface

IT IS NOW ABOUT thirty years since I finished work on the Word commentary on Genesis 1–15. So I welcomed the invitation to give the 2013 Didsbury lectures at the Nazarene College in Manchester as an opportunity to review and clarify ideas I had expressed in the commentary. Has the third millennium made obsolete the insights of the second? This is why I entitled the lectures enshrined in this book *Rethinking Genesis 1–11*.

Those who have read the commentary attentively will I hope agree that my interpretation of these opening chapters of Scripture has not altered substantially. I have tweaked the arguments here and there, but there are no great theological U-turns to excite reviewers and heresy hunters!

But this short volume does, by virtue of its brevity, have one great advantage over its predecessor: it focuses clearly on the central ideas of Genesis, whereas in my commentary some of these points are liable to get lost in the technical details so often regarded as central in major commentary series. The great message of these opening chapters of Genesis is obscured by a variety of debates. Issues about sources, dating, authorship, and historical and scientific accuracy easily sidetrack the reader, so that he or she forgets that this is Scripture, the word of God for both ancient and modern readers.

It is the argument of this book that Genesis 1–11 sets out with vivid clarity some of the key theological principles of the Bible, from the unity and sovereignty of the Creator to the importance of the Sabbath and marriage. It shows and teaches the pervasiveness and depth of sin and portrays its dire consequences. It pictures a God who demands complete obedience to his laws, yet who is amazingly long-suffering and forgiving of mankind's sinful ways. These themes, set out so simply and clearly in Genesis 1–11, run through later parts of Scripture. In this way Genesis 1–11 can provide us with the theological spectacles with which to read the Bible both sympathetically and appropriately. More than that, it gives us a vision of God's purposes for creation and man's place in the divine scheme. Its principles provide a framework of thought for interpreting our present world, both its glories and its problems. Like Saint Augustine we are invited to "take up and read." If we do so, and allow its biblical truths to embed themselves in our souls, these chapters of Genesis have the potential to transform us as individuals, as a society, and eventually our world.

November 22, 2014

1

Rethinking Genesis 1
A Creation Designed for Man

Introduction

FEW BIBLICAL TEXTS ARE the focus of such controversy as Genesis 1–11.[1] Anyone setting out to read the Bible is immediately plunged into difficulty with the very first chapters. And assumptions about the nature of the text brought by the reader will profoundly determine how it is understood. The scientist who reads it like an article in *Nature* or the *New Scientist* will read it quite differently from the anthropologist who classifies it as primitive myth. Within the Christian community, creationists will see the opening chapters of Genesis as literal history, while theistic evolutionists will understand them as theological narrative.

On reflection, we can see that each interpreter comes with his own agenda and then tries to give an interpretation compatible with his preconceptions. And anyone who points this out is liable to find himself making the same mistakes. Can we escape the vicious circle and instead of imposing our own interpretation on the text allow the text to speak for itself? This is the great problem of hermeneutics, discussed at length in numerous books and articles.

This book will not enter into this debate at a theoretical level. It must suffice to say that I do not agree with those who think that it is so difficult

---

1. I thank Dr. Robin A. Parry for his helpful comments on my text.

to avoid subjective interpretation that we cannot understand the author's meaning, at least approximately. With careful attention to the ancient Near Eastern context in which the text originated, it is possible to define the genres used in Genesis 1–11 and thereby attune ourselves to the message that was intended to be conveyed. But it is not just ancient Near Eastern texts that can be drawn on to illuminate Genesis. Literary criticism, which pays close attention to the shape and structure of texts, also provides invaluable insights into its meaning. Using these methods and the insights of commentators ancient and modern, I shall endeavor to draw out the meaning of the text as it was understood 3,000 years ago, a meaning that still resonates with us today.

Genesis 1

Some Earlier Commentators

The opening chapter of Genesis is majestic as it declares God's sovereign power in ordering the cosmos. Repeatedly God says, "Let there be X," and the narrator reports, "And there was X." In just six days of working, God brings the whole world into being. This pattern is obvious to every reader of Genesis, but how have commentators understood these days of divine activity?

According to Saint Augustine (354–430 AD), probably the most influential Christian theologian of all time, God created the universe out of nothing, but he doubts whether this was done in six ordinary days. "What kind of days these were it is extremely difficult, or perhaps impossible, for us to conceive."[2] He goes on to point out that the first three days of creation must be different from days four to six, because the sun was not created until the fourth day. "We see that our ordinary days have no evening but by the setting, and no morning but by the rising of the sun; but the first three days of all were passed without sun, since it was reported to have been made on the fourth day."[3]

Similarly John Calvin, the great Protestant reformer and Bible commentator, rejects the theory that held God created everything in a moment: rather he did not hurry, but took six days. But that is not to say that Calvin regards Genesis 1 as a scientific account. He says: "He who would learn

2. Augustine, *City of God*, 11.6.
3. Ibid., 11.7.

astronomy and other recondite arts, let him go elsewhere"[4] Rather, he sees Genesis as written for the unlearned, and it therefore does not offer an exact account, but describes how things appear to the simple observer. Calvin knows that there is not an ocean above the firmament of the heaven, but that is how it seems when it rains. The windows of heaven open and water gushes out. Calvin thus sees the division of God's creative activity into six working days as an accommodation to human nature: it would overwhelm the human reader to have all God's creative acts occurring on the same day.[5]

The distinguished nineteenth-century commentator Franz Delitzsch argued that the days were days in the life of God and therefore could be of any length as measured by human standards. "Days of God are intended, and with Him a thousand years are but as a day that is past, Ps.xc.4." Those who argue "that the days of creation are, according to the meaning of Holy Scripture itself, not days of four-and-twenty hours, but aeons, are perfectly right."[6]

With Hermann Gunkel's (1862–1930) *Schöpfung und Chaos in Urzeit und Endzeit*[7] (1895) and his commentary on Genesis (1901) the modern era in the study of Genesis 1–11 began. Gunkel was the first to seriously engage with the material from Mesopotamia that archaeologists were unearthing and assyriologists were deciphering. He focused on the story of the cosmic battle between the gods Marduk and Tiamat, which is described in *Enuma elish*. He argued that there were echoes of this conflict in the Bible, especially in the Psalms and Isaiah, and that it formed the background to Genesis 1. However, he thought that in the Old Testament the major mythical features have been expunged and now we can talk only of "faded myth."[8] The same general position is taken by Gerhard von Rad and Claus Westermann in their great Genesis commentaries. While they both acknowledge parallels between Genesis 1 and other Near Eastern texts, they pointedly refrain from describing Genesis 1–11 as myth. Von Rad says "In essence [Genesis 1] is not myth and not saga, but Priestly doctrine."[9]

---

4. Calvin, *Commentary on Genesis*, 79.
5. Ibid., 78.
6. Delitzsch, *Commentary on Genesis*, 84.
7. The English translation is *Creation and Chaos in the Primeval Era and the Eschaton*.
8. Gunkel, *Creation and Chaos*, 80, 82.
9. von Rad, *Genesis*, 63.

And Westermann regularly refers to the opening chapters of Genesis as "story" or "narrative."[10]

Literary Patterns

This rapid survey shows the diversity of approach to the first chapter in the Bible and it invites us to take a fresh look at some of the issues, particularly using the tools of literary analysis to see if there are any clues to its genre. These investigations will show that it is a highly structured and artistic piece of literature. It has long been observed that the six days of creation are paired: that though the first three days must have differed from the last three because there was no sun to define the first group, the first day corresponds to the fourth, the second to the fifth, and the third to the sixth.

Day 1. Creation of Light	Day 4. Creation of Lights = Sun, Moon, Stars
Day 2. Creation of Sky and Sea	Day 5. Creation of Birds of Air and Fish of Sea
Day 3. Creation of Land and Plants	Day 6. Creation of Animals and Man
Day 7. Sabbath	

Not only does day 3 correspond to day 6 in what is created, the creation of the land and plants makes possible the life of man and the animals.

The failure to pair the Sabbath with another day makes it unique. It stands apart, not only in content (God rests instead of working), but also in structure.

If 2:1–3 is the tailpiece to the six days of divine activity, 1:1–2 is the prelude. The great Jewish commentator Cassuto drew attention to the way prelude and tailpiece have common features that bespeak careful composition. For example, the wording of 1:1 is echoed in 2:1–2, but the key terms appear in reverse order. Literally translated 1:1 reads "In the beginning created God the heavens and the earth." "Created," "God," and "heavens and earth" reappear in 2:1–3.

---

10. Westermann, *Genesis 1–11*, 1–5.

2:3 God rested from all his work ... in *creation*

2:2 On the seventh day *God* finished

2:1 *the heavens and the earth* were finished

This inversion of key terms makes a clever inclusion and brings the account to a firm conclusion. But it is not the only linkage between the opening and closing verses of 1:1 to 2:3. They are both made up of multiples of seven words. 1:1 has seven words, 1:2 has fourteen (7 x 2) words, while 2:1–3 has thirty-five (7 x 5) words. This suggests that the number 7 has special significance for the author of Genesis 1: it heralds the frequent association of this number with holy activities, especially in rituals. The circling of Jericho on seven days, and seven times on the seventh day, headed by seven priests with seven trumpets is a striking example of this (Joshua 6). Not only is the seventh day of the week holy, but so too are the seventh month of the year and the seventh year (Lev 23:23–43; 25:8–22). In various rituals certain gestures are repeated seven times.[11]

This makes it likely that it is not a coincidence that 1:1–2 and 2:1–3 are multiples of 7. The probability that it is deliberate is heightened when it is noted that several key terms or phrases in the chapter also occur in multiples of 7. "God" occurs thirty-five times, "earth" twenty-one times, "heaven/firmament" twenty-one times, and the phrases "and it was so" and "God saw that it was good" occur seven times each.

The intricacy of the verbal patterns becomes even more striking when the phrases associated with the individual acts of creation are examined. Eight acts of creation are accomplished in six days. This is achieved by doubling the acts of creation on days three and six. On day three land and plants are created (vv. 9–13) and on day six the animals and man are created (vv. 24–31). This enhances the parallels between the first three days and the second three days. But the careful patterning does not end here.

Each day begins with the narrator introducing the divine command with "And God said" (vv. 3, 6, 9, 11, 14, 20, 24, 26, 28, 29), a total of ten times. This is followed eight times by the command, "let there be ..." (vv. 3, 6, 9, 11, 14, 20, 24, 26). Then seven times comes the fulfillment formula, "And it was so" (vv. 3, 7, 9, 11, 15, 24, 30), the execution formula, "And God made" (vv. 4, 7, 12, 16, 21, 25, 27), the approval formula, "And God saw that it was good" (vv. 4, 10, 12, 18, 21, 25, 31), a divine word of naming or blessing (vv. 5 [x2], 8, 10 [x2], 22, 28), and the mention of the days (vv. 5, 8, 13,

---

11. E.g., Lev 8:11; 14:7–9; 2 Kgs 5:10.

19, 23, 31; 2:2). The concentration of groups of seven is striking. Although there are ten announcements of divine speech and eight commands cited, all the formulae are grouped in sevens, requiring the fulfillment formula to be omitted in v. 20, the execution formula in v. 9, and the approval formula in vv. 6–8.

These observations about the structure of the opening chapter of Genesis show that it is a carefully composed piece of work, not a casually written account of creation. The deliberation of the author in structuring this overture to Genesis echoes the deliberation of the Creator in structuring the world. It seems to imply that poetic demands are at least as important as historical considerations in the composition of this chapter. In particular, it demonstrates the great significance of the number 7 throughout the opening of Genesis. While the modern reader tends to view God's works on the first six days as of most importance, the symbolism of 7 directs the reader's attention to the seventh day, God's day of rest.

But are there any more clues to the nature of Genesis 1? We should, of course, ask how it relates to the rest of the book, as often the key ideas in a work are expressed most clearly in its prologue. However, before we address this issue it is essential to ask how it compares to other ancient texts from the Near East, from places such as Mesopotamia, Egypt, Ugarit and Ebla in Syria, and the Hittite empire in Turkey. All these ancient cultures had stories of origins, but by far the best-documented are the myths of Mesopotamia.[12] Most pertinent to the understanding of Genesis 1–11 are the Atrahasis epic, the Gilgamesh epic, and *Enuma elish*, often dubbed the Epic of Creation.

Mesopotamian Parallels to Genesis 1–11

Enuma elish

Ever since Gunkel's study *Creation and Chaos in the Primeval Era and the Eschaton*[13] drew attention to some similarities between *Enuma elish* and Genesis, much debate has centered on the relationship between the two texts. Recent scholarship has tended to think that the connection has been overstated. Nevertheless, in *Enuma elish* Marduk, the hero god of the story,

---

12. Conveniently translated in Dalley, *Myths from Mesopotamia*.

13. Originally published in German as *Schöpfung und Chaos in Urzeit und Endzeit* in 1895, but not translated into English till 2006.

does demonstrate his power by various acts of creation, but these are marginal to the main thrust of the work, whereas Genesis 1 offers a systematic and focused account of the creation of the heavens and earth. *Enuma elish*, on the other hand, is more a biography of Marduk, the chief god of Babylon, explaining how he became number 1 in the Babylonian pantheon. It tells of his birth from the god Ea and the goddess Damkina and how he rose to supreme power. The pantheon is portrayed as a large extended family, most of whose members are related to each other in some way. But it is an unhappy family: the older generation falls out with the younger gods. This civil war climaxes with the old goddess Tiamat and her supporters trying to annihilate the younger generation of gods. But Ea, the god of magic and the underworld and leader of the younger generation, finds his magic powerless against the all-conquering Tiamat, so Marduk ventures to take her on in single combat. He traps her in his net, inflates her with wind so that she cannot shut her mouth, and shoots an arrow down her throat. It enters her heart and she dies. Marduk leaps on her corpse, cuts it in two, and uses one part to make the sky and the other to make the earth.

Having proved his supremacy by the conquest of Tiamat, Marduk appointed the moon and the sun to govern the weekly, monthly, and annual calendar. He also declared his purpose to turn Babylon into a holy city by building a great temple there, one of whose roles was to serve as a hotel and conference centre for those times when the gods descend to earth. As a result of the great battle some of the gods were relieved of their duties of feeding the great gods and Marduk commissioned his father Ea to create man. This was done by executing Qingu, Tiamat's chief adviser and general, and making mankind out of his blood. In gratitude for Marduk freeing them from Tiamat's domination and their duty as food purveyors to the great gods, the lesser gods built the great Esagila temple in Babylon. The epic concludes with listing Marduk's fifty names, which children had to learn, together with an explanation of each name. These names usually celebrated one of his feats in battle.

It is therefore clear that the epic has two major purposes: 1) to justify Marduk's place as head god in Babylon and 2) to make the claim for Babylon's status as the holy city. This is why the epic was recited at least once a year on the fourth day of the New Year festival. In other words, Marduk's acts of creation are quite marginal to the main thrust of the epic. Nevertheless, we need to take a closer look at his creative activity to assess its relevance to Genesis.

It was after Marduk had slain Tiamat that he turned his attention to the stars, moon, and sun and gave them the job of marking the seasons, years, months, and weeks. He began with the signs of the Zodiac:

> As for the stars, he set constellations corresponding to them.
> He designated the year and marked out its divisions,
> Apportioned three stars each to the twelve months (*Enuma* 5:2–4)[14]

Then in great detail the functions of the moon are described:

> He made the crescent moon appear, entrusted night to it,
> And designated it the jewel of night to mark out the days. (*Enuma* 5:12–13)[15]

There then follow precise instructions to the moon on how to wax and wane on different days of the month and how to keep in step with the sun's movements. The seventh, fifteenth, and thirtieth days of the month are specially mentioned. But Shamash, the sun god, is noted for being responsible only for the year.

After this the other gods acclaim Marduk as king. Though he is one of the youngest gods, they now are ready to make him their boss. "Previously the Lord [i.e., Marduk] was our beloved Son, but now he is our king. We shall take heed of his command" (*Enuma* 5:end).[16] This gives Marduk an idea on how to relieve the lesser gods of their toil.

> Let me put blood together, and make bones too.
> Let me set up primeval man: Man shall be his name. (*Enuma* 6:5–6)[17]

However, it is not Marduk who created man, but Marduk's father, Ea. Ea puts the proposal to the other gods, offering them increased leisure if man was created to undertake their work. But it required a god to die if man was to be made of a god's blood, and Ea recommended that Qingu, the god who directed Tiamat's campaign, should be executed.

> Let one who is hostile to them [the gods] be surrendered up
> Let him be destroyed, and let people be created [from him]. (*Enuma elish* 6:13–14)[18]

14. Dalley, *Myths from Mesopotamia*, 255.
15. Ibid., 256.
16. Ibid., 260.
17. Ibid., 260.
18. Ibid., 261.

This proposal was well received. So Qingu was arrested:

> They bound him and held him in front of Ea,
> Imposed the penalty on him and cut off his blood.
> He created mankind from his blood
> Imposed the toil of the gods on man and released the gods from it. (*Enuma elish* 6:31–34)[19]

The gods were so grateful to be relieved of their earthly chores that they offered to build a shrine for Marduk in Babylon:

> Now, O Lord, that you have set us free,
> What are our favours from you?
> We would like to make a shrine with its own name.
> We would like our night's resting place to be in your private quarters, and to rest there. (*Enuma elish* 6:49–52)[20]

> When Marduk heard this,
> His face lit up greatly, like daylight.
> Create Babylon, whose construction you requested! (*Enuma elish* 6:55–57)[21]

It took the gods two years to build this great temple of Esagila, and when it was completed they celebrated by holding a banquet.

> The Lord invited the gods his fathers to attend a banquet
> In the great sanctuary which he had created as his dwelling.
> He told them to celebrate.
> "Indeed, Bab-ili is your home too!
> Sing for joy there, dwell in happiness!"
> The great gods sat down there,
> And set out the beer mugs; they attended the banquet
> When they had made merry within,
> They themselves made a *taqribtu* offering in splendid Esagila. (*Enuma elish* 6:71–77)[22]

---

19. Ibid.
20. Ibid., 262.
21. Ibid.
22. Ibid., 263.

They offered a sacrifice and allocated themselves their particular roles in the cosmos. The great gods made Marduk king and then swore an oath of allegiance to him. The epic then ends by recalling Marduk's fifty names and giving a short explanation of each one. These names are supposed to recall Marduk's heroic achievements related earlier in the epic and to remind people that he is the one who makes agriculture successful. One of the names recalls his creation of mankind and the relief this brought to the gods who had labored hitherto.

Enuma elish thus has some parallels to Genesis. Besides recounting the creation of the sun, moon, and stars, and later the creation of man, *Enuma elish* begins with describing the mixing of the salt-water and sweet-water oceans represented by Tiamat and her husband Apsu. It was their mixing together that created the other gods in Tiamat's womb. This has been compared with Genesis 1:2, which speaks of darkness covering the waters. But this minor similarity should alert us to the very different atmosphere of Genesis 1 and *Enuma elish*. Genesis has only one God, not a brood of gods and goddesses, the products of divine sexual congress. Whereas Genesis focuses on creation, *Enuma elish* is chiefly concerned with the struggles between the gods for supremacy—the creation of the heavenly bodies is almost incidental. Whereas Genesis portrays a cosmos being prepared as a hospitable home for man, and the creation of the human race as the triumphant climax of the Creator's efforts, in *Enuma elish* it is merely a sideshow, and though man's creation was Marduk's idea, it was Ea, father of Marduk, who carried it out. In other words, the creation of mankind does not have the significance it has in Genesis. By contrast, in Genesis creation is both God's idea and his achievement.

Genesis could be reacting to the polytheistic theogonies of which *Enuma elish* is an example, but it seems unlikely that it is rejecting the specific features of *Enuma elish*. As Wilfred Lambert pointed out,[23] *Enuma elish* does not represent normative Mesopotamian creation mythology—indeed on some datings of the two texts, *Enuma elish* could be contemporary with the composition of Genesis or even a little later. It is in the Atrahasis epic (composed no later than 1700 BC) that we have an expression of mainstream Babylonian beliefs and closer parallels with Genesis.

---

23. Lambert, "New Look at the Babylonian Background to Genesis," 107.

The Atrahasis Epic

The Atrahasis epic begins not with the birth of various gods, ancestors of Marduk, but with the Igigi gods toiling to produce food for their superiors:

> When the gods instead of man
> Did the work, bore the loads,
> The gods' load was too great,
> The work too hard, the trouble too much.
> The gods had to dig out canals,
> Had to clear channels, the lifelines of the land.
> The gods dug out the Tigris riverbed
> And then dug out the Euphrates. (*Atrahasis* 1:1–4, 21–22, 25–26)[24]

After working 3,600 years they decided to protest to Enlil, the great god in charge. They set fire to their tools and surrounded Enlil's dwelling. He was asleep because it was late at night and he had to be woken by his gatekeeper Nusku. Enlil then summoned the other top gods, and one of them, Ea, advised compromise:

> Belet-ili the womb-goddess is present—
> Let her create primeval man
> So that he may bear the yoke.
> Let man bear the load of the gods. (*Atrahasis* 1)[25]

So under Ea's supervision man was created. A god called Ilawela was killed and its blood mixed with clay. From this mixture seven human couples were molded by fourteen womb-goddesses, who acted as midwives. In this way the creation of these first human couples anticipated all future human births and provided a precedent and a model for future births and the role of the midwife.

Six hundred years passed, mankind multiplied, and the noise of their activities disturbed the great gods. So Enlil addressed the great gods:

> The noise of mankind has become too much
> I am losing sleep over their racket.
> Give the order that *shuruppu*-disease shall break out. (*Atrahasis* II)[26]

---

24. Dalley, *Myths from Mesopotamia*, 9.
25. Ibid., 14.
26. Ibid., 23.

Then began a plague that decimated the human race, the first of several divine attempts to limit human population growth. These attempts climaxed in the flood, of which more subsequently.

It is the way that the Atrahasis epic connects creation and flood that makes it such an interesting parallel to Genesis. Its initial focus on the creation of man is also striking, as that is the climax of Genesis 1, while the use of clay as an ingredient of human beings has similarities with the creation of Adam from the dust of the ground in Genesis 2.

But again there are striking differences between the two accounts. Firstly, there is only *one* God in Genesis, not the extended family of gods and goddesses in Atrahasis. And while Atrahasis highlights the creation of man, it comes in a very different context. Most of Genesis 1 tells of the preparation of the environment to make it suitable for human habitation. The creation of those features essential to human life, the seasons, dry land, plants, and animals are all described in Genesis before man is created. Indeed mankind is given the plants to eat by God, whereas in Atrahasis and *Enuma elish* man is made to relieve the minor gods of laboring to irrigate the land and to produce food for the high gods. The Mesopotamian gods often find themselves at loggerheads, indeed engage in mortal combat, whereas Genesis 1 portrays a world at peace. This is not only because there are no other gods to quarrel with the Almighty, but because both man and the animals are vegetarian, there is no animal slaughter. Instead, God gives them the plants to eat. So there is no need to kill to eat or to kill for any other reason. Genesis 1 thus posits a world without violence. This first emerges as a problem in 3:15, with the woman's son and the serpent's offspring bruising each other. Violence becomes a major problem in Genesis 4 when Cain kills his brother. It becomes endemic in 6:11 and 13, which declare "the earth was filled with violence," a situation so incompatible with the original creation that God decides to destroy the world in a flood and start again with a new creation.

This approach is strikingly different from *Enuma elish* and *Atrahasis*. Genesis seems to be rejecting the Mesopotamian accounts in order to portray a different vision of the universe. There is but one God, not numerous gods and goddesses. The divine plan was for peace not discord. The world was designed for human habitation, not as a place for the gods to visit. The creation of the heavenly bodies also served this end, not as a demonstration of one god's superiority over his rivals. The one God provided man with food, not the other way round. In *Atrahasis* the story of man's creation is not an explanation of his role, so much as that of midwives in assisting birth.

John Walton's Approach

Recently John Walton[27] has developed a new approach to the creation stories of the ancient Near East. He points out that in many accounts the emphasis is not on creating the material heaven and earth, but on commissioning the different gods and other creatures to do their job. The moon, for instance, is authorized to wax and wane to mark the passing of the seasons (e.g., *Enuma elish* 5:12–22). Furthermore, *Enuma elish* climaxes with the making of the temple of Marduk in Babylon for the god to dwell in. Walton sees the same pattern in Genesis 1. He argues that God's creative acts are not *making* the water and the firmament, light and darkness, plants and animals, *but assigning them roles*. The firmament separates the water above the earth from that below the earth. The heavenly bodies rule the night and the day. Mankind is appointed to reproduce and to rule as God's image on earth. When all this has been done, God rests on the seventh day in his created world, his temple on earth. The process took seven days, for that was the ancient conventional timespan for dedicating temples.

While it is certainly true that some of the divine fiats in Genesis institute the active roles of light, the land, the heavenly bodies, and so forth, it would seem to be going too far to argue that no material creation was involved. The creation of the firmament, plants, and animals, and even man (more clear in Genesis 2 and *Enuma elish* and *Atrahasis*) definitely seem to involve a divine manufacturing process. This need not involve creation *ex nihilo*, but in some cases that may be implied. More convincing is Walton's[28] likening the creation of the world to the building of a temple. The world is not merely designed for human habitation, but as God's own dwelling place. God and man are intended to live together in total harmony.

Genesis 1–11 may be seen to set out the fundamental theological and ethical assumptions that are presupposed in the rest of Scripture. For the ancient readers it distinguishes Israelite faith from the beliefs of their contemporaries in neighboring lands. For modern readers these chapters can do the same. They provide, as it were, exegetical spectacles for the reader,

---

27. Walton, *Genesis 1 as Ancient Cosmology*; Walton, *Lost World of Genesis 1*.

28. Already suggested by Weinfeld in "Sabbath, Temple and the Enthronement of the LORD."

so that when he or she reads about God in subsequent narratives or poetry he will bring to the text the picture of God and his ways portrayed in the opening chapters of Genesis.

The Contribution of Genesis 1

What then, we may ask, is the particular contribution of Genesis 1? The first and fundamental point it makes is that *there is only one God*. This vision stands in contrast to the rest of the ancient world, which held there were a multitude of gods and goddesses, each with his or her own sphere of influence. For example, the sun and moon were seen as gods in their own right, but in Genesis the words "sun" and "moon" are not used, lest they be understood to refer to the sun god and the moon god. Instead, Genesis speaks of "the greater light" and "the lesser light." Because there is only one God, Genesis lacks the stories of gods mating and producing children. There are also no battles between the gods, such as fill the verses of *Enuma elish*. The God of Genesis is unique and without rivals. He is not, however, the only spiritual being in the universe. Genesis 1:26 says, "Let *us* make man in *our* image, after *our* likeness." Why does God use the plural, us and our, and not the singular, me and my? Why did he not say, "Let *me* create man in *my* image, after *my* likeness"? Gunkel argued that the use of the plural was a hangover from polytheistic ideas. Jews have held that the plural refers to angels, while Christians see this as adumbrating the Trinity. It is not necessary to decide between these options to see that, whichever view one takes, Genesis holds that the Supreme God is not alone. There are other beings who can admire his chief handiwork, man. 6:1–4 confirms this when it mentions the sons of God. This phrase also found in Job 1–2, where we find members of the divine council reporting back to God on their activities. In some of the psalms these beings are simply called "gods." In Psalm 97:7 they are summoned to praise: "worship him, all you gods." But though they may be called gods, they are totally subservient to the only one who deserves that title, "For the LORD is a great God, and a great King above all gods" (Ps 95:3 cf. 96:4–5).

The main difference between the Great God and the other spiritual beings, the so-called "gods," is sovereignty. The God of Genesis displays almighty power. All earth's domains are under his total control, the light, the waters, the land and plant life, the sun, moon, and stars, the sea and the air, the animals and man. All are under his control and mandated to fulfill specific roles. Whereas in Mesopotamian thought these things were decided by negotiations between the gods, in Genesis the one almighty God simply announces his will and it happens.

Another striking feature of Genesis 1 is the role it assigns to man. In ancient Near Eastern thought mankind was created to relieve the gods of the toil of agriculture: in Genesis it is the other way round. In fact, the works of the first five days may be seen as essentially providing an environment in which man could flourish. This is particularly obvious in the establishment of dry land, the appointment of sun and moon to determine the seasons, and the growth of plants and fruit trees to provide mankind with food. Here God's goodwill towards humanity is particularly plain.

But it is the description of mankind's creation that really brings out God's pride in this culmination of the creative process. We have already noted how God invites other heavenly beings to observe and perhaps even participate in the creation of man, when he says: "let us make man in our image." By describing mankind as the "image of God," the Creator is assigning a unique status to the human race: its many members are God's representatives on earth, given the duty of managing the rest of creation for God. This is why they are instructed: "Be fruitful and multiply and fill the earth and subdue it, and have dominion over the fish of the sea and over the birds of the heavens and over every living thing that moves on the earth" (1:28). Filling the earth and subduing it is not a license to exploit the earth's resources selfishly but to utilize them responsibly for the mutual good of mankind and the environment. This follows from man being in the divine image, for God rules his creation benevolently, and on the first five days of creation organized it for man's welfare. In ancient oriental thought, kings were often seen as representing the gods, in this way legitimizing their rule over other humans. But Genesis declares that *every* man and woman is made in the image of God and is therefore responsible for playing a role in filling the earth and managing it. As divine representatives they are expected to do this in a godlike way; that is, for the benefit of the whole race, not just for particular groups and interests.

To achieve this goal of creation management there is a need of workers, so this is why humanity is told to be fruitful and multiply. Propagation of humans is thus central to the divine plan, hence the deliberate highlighting of maleness and femaleness, which is consequent on man's creation in the divine image.

So

> God created man in his own image,
> in the image of God he created him;
> male and female he created them. (Gen 1:27)

This positive attitude to human reproduction contrasts with mainstream Babylonian thought, which sees man's creation as a divine afterthought, which the gods subsequently regretted and did their best to curtail by plague, drought, and flood. But for Genesis the creation of humans is the *climax* to God's work in creation.

However, the creation of humans is not the *goal* of creation: its goal is the divine rest on the seventh day. We have already noticed the propensity of temple-building texts to conclude with the deity coming to rest in the sanctuary on the seventh day. And it seems likely that Genesis echoes this pattern. Creating the cosmos is like building a shrine for God: he intended to dwell on earth with man. Though subsequent chapters of Genesis record the frustration of this plan, it is important to recognize the divine intention. This ideal of rest and harmony hangs together with the implied vegetarianism of man and beast indicated by God assigning them the plants to eat. Peace between all God's creatures and the divine presence on earth is the essence of the divine scheme.

But it is not simply a harmonious universe that Genesis 1 portrays. God's work in creation takes six days and then he rests on the seventh. Man is created in the divine image, which means he is supposed to imitate God's activity in certain respects, in this context most obviously by working for six days and resting on the seventh. This is implicit in Genesis and explicit in Exodus 20.

> Remember the Sabbath day to keep it holy. Six days you shall labor and do all your work. . . . For in six days the LORD made heaven and earth, the sea, and all that is in them, and rested the seventh day. Therefore the LORD blessed the Sabbath day and made it holy. (Exod 20:8, 9, 11)

The length of the Sabbath commandment, the longest of the Ten, witnesses to the importance of the Sabbath in biblical thinking. Genesis 1 underlines the significance of the Sabbath by showing how God created the universe in six days and then rested. Indeed, one might describe Genesis 1 as an etiology of the Sabbath, i.e., an explanation of its origin and significance.

Conclusion

It is now time to sum up our investigation into Genesis 1. I have tried to allow it to speak for itself by examining its literary form and by comparing it with other ancient Near Eastern texts on similar topics. Our first finding was that it is a brilliantly composed introduction to Genesis and the rest of the Old Testament. It provides us with the exegetical spectacles to read the rest of Genesis sympathetically. Its emphasis on the number 7 in various details makes its description of God resting on the seventh day particularly significant: if God rests on the seventh day, so should man, made in his image.

Second, many of the features of the Genesis narrative, such as what God creates and the structure of the texts, find striking parallels in non-biblical literature, especially Mesopotamian myths and epics. But an ancient oriental from outside Israel encountering Genesis 1 for the first time would be particularly struck by the *differences* between the theology of Genesis and the usual Near Eastern beliefs. Here we meet just one all-powerful God, who speaks and what he commands comes to pass, not a multitude of competing gods and goddesses, each with his or her own sphere of influence. Also, unlike most oriental divinities, this God views the creation of mankind as the summit of divine creativity, not a mere incident in the history of the world. In fact, Genesis holds that *all* mankind is in the image of God, not just royalty, and that *every* human has the privilege and duty of managing creation on God's behalf. Orientals believed man's role was to sustain the gods, so that they did not go hungry. Genesis holds that to be an illusion: rather God cares for man by providing him with the plants as his food.

In these ways, Genesis 1 sketches an outline biblical theology. Monotheism and divine sovereignty are fundamental in that theology. So too is the place of man in the divine economy. God's concern with human welfare is also a striking feature of this opening chapter of the Bible. It does not take much imagination to project these ideas forward and see their ultimate fulfillment in the doctrines of the Trinity and the Incarnation. But of that, more in the next chapter.

2

Rethinking Genesis 2–4

Creation Disrupted by Man

Introduction

In the last chapter we endeavored to orient ourselves to the leading ideas of Genesis 1 by two approaches: first, we looked at the way the chapter was intricately structured so that the number 7 and the seventh day were highlighted, and second, we compared Genesis 1 with other ancient accounts of creation, such as *Enuma elish* and the Atrahasis epic, which we suggested might help us to read Genesis as the first readers did. We noted the clear monotheistic emphasis of Genesis, with one supreme God creating and sustaining the heavens and earth. This creation is designed for man, whom God supplies with food, rather than the other way round, with man producing food for the gods as Babylonians held. But the universe is also intended to be a super temple, where God should dwell in harmony with his creatures. In this way Genesis sets out the presuppositions that should guide the reader of the subsequent chapters. Genesis 1 thus provides the exegetical spectacles by whose aid one should read the rest of the book.

2:4, Title of 2:4—4:26

The first chapter (more precisely 1:1—2:3) is set off from the rest of the book by a heading in 2:4, which is similar to nine further headings in the rest of

Rethinking Genesis 2-4

the book. "This is the history of . . ." ("these are the generations of . . .") heralds each new section of Genesis, either a genealogy (5:1; 10:1; 11:10; 25:12; 36:1) or a long narrative (2:4, Adam and Eve; 6:9, the flood; 11:27, Abraham; 25:19, Jacob; 37:2, Joseph). This heading in 2:4 thus serves to link the Garden of Eden story (2:5—4:16) with the flood story and the biographies of the patriarchs, *not* with the opening chapter (1:1—2:3), which stands aloof from what follows. Westermann[1] has termed it the overture to what follows. But as we analyze what follows 2:3, we shall see it contains some themes and motifs that are not found in the overture. It reinforces God's concern for man's welfare in the provision of a well-stocked garden, but it introduces the concept of sin and discloses the world being engulfed in an avalanche of violence. These chapters reiterate the absolute supremacy of the creator, but chapter 3 introduces the serpent, a malign figure of opposition to the Creator. To these issues we shall return in due course, but first we must examine the structure of chapters 2–4 and investigate possible antecedents to them in Near Eastern literature.

The Structure of Genesis 2–4

I have asserted that the formula "This is the history of . . ." links the material in 2:4—4:26 with the major narratives that follow, suggesting that the ancient readers regarded the story of Adam and Eve in much the same way as they viewed the tales of the patriarchs. However, there is a difference between these headings. 2:4 is fuller and more elaborate than the other headings. Compare 2:4 with 6:9.

> These are the generations of the heavens and the earth
> > When they were created
> > In the day that the LORD God made
> The earth and the heavens.
> (Gen 2:4)

> These are the generations of Noah.
> (Gen 6:9)

Not only is 2:4 longer than the title in 6:9, but it is a more intricately constructed chiasm, with "when they were created" matching "in the day that

---

1. Westermann, *Genesis 1–11*, 93.

the LORD God made." And "the heavens and the earth" matching "the earth and the heavens." This last phrase—"earth and heavens"[2]—is particularly striking in inverting the normal word order "heavens and earth." This inversion suggests it is a deliberate attempt to enhance the chiastic structure. But this elaborate title to the following narratives also serves as a link to the opening verse of Genesis. "In the beginning God created the heavens and the earth" is echoed by "the heavens and the earth when they were created," while the two verbs "create" and "make" are the terms repeatedly used of God's activity in chapter 1. Thus chapters 2-4 are set off from chapter 1 on the one hand and chapter 5 on the other by the titles "This is the history of . . ." / "This is the book of the history of . . ." in 2:4 and 5:1, yet they are, by these same titles, linked with the adjacent materials. In other words, these titles show that 2:4—4:26 is the first main section in the Genesis narrative.

Elements in Genesis 2:4—4:26

But examining 2:4—4:26 we find that it contains a variety of material:

2:4—3:24	The first human couple
4:1-16	The first murder
4:17-24	The first craftsmen
4:25-26	The first descendants of Seth

The last two verses anticipate the next chapter, which is a genealogy from Adam to Noah down the line of Seth. We could describe 4:25-26 as introducing chapter 5. 4:25 tells of the birth of Eve's son Seth and verse 26 of the grandson Enosh (cf. 5:3-11). In other words, 4:25-26 serve as a trailer for chapter 5. This use of a trailer at the end of one section to prepare the reader for the next is characteristic of Genesis. For example, 6:5-8 analyses the problem of the human heart, intimates God's intention to wipe out mankind, but notes the righteousness of Noah. In this way it serves as a precursor of the flood narrative (6:9—9:29; cf. 9:18-29; 11:26; 25:11).

Careful organization is also evident in the remainder of chapters 2-4. Though chapter 2 is often seen as an alternative creation story, closer

---

2. The only other use is in Ps 148:13, which appears to quote Gen 2:4.

Rethinking Genesis 2–4

observation shows that it really is giving the background for the decisive events in chapter 3. Chapters 2–3 fall into seven scenes.

1. 2:5–17. Narrative describing the creation of the garden and man's role in it

   2. 2:18–25. Narrative describing the creation of the animals and the woman

      3. 3:1–5. Dialogue between the snake and the woman

         4. 3:6–8. Narrative about the woman and the man

      5. 3:9–13. Dialogue between God, the man, and the woman

   6. 3:14–21. Narrative describing the disruption of creation relationships

7. 3:22–24. Narrative describing the human couple leaving the garden

This is another chiastic structure, with scene 1 matching scene 7, scene 2 matching scene 6, scene 3 matching scene 5, while scene 4 stands alone representing the turning point in the episode when the couple take of the forbidden fruit, their eyes open, and they realize their nakedness.

Chapter 4:1–16 describes an even more serious sin than Adam's. Cain's slaughter of his brother is a particularly heinous murder, for brothers are supposed to look out for each other, not slay each other. It is evident from the subject matter that this tale represents a further decline in the behavior of humans, but this perception is enhanced by the parallels between chapter 4 and chapter 3.

Like chapters 2–3, 4:1–16 is organized chiastically,[3] but more interestingly it echoes the phraseology of the preceding chapters. In 3:9 God summons Adam with the words, "Where are you?" In 4:9 God asks Cain, "Where is Abel your brother?" In both stories the divine interrogation continues: "What [is this that] you have done?" (3:13; 4:10). In both the ground is cursed (3:17; 4:11). Both stories conclude with the human actors being driven eastwards from God's presence (3:24; 4:16). Another connection between the accounts is in the rare word translated "desire" in 3:16 and 4:7.

But there are also intriguing differences between Genesis 2–3 and chapter 4 showing that the latter is not just an alternative account of a sin that separates man from God. Cain's attitude as well as his action are worse than those of Adam and Eve. Whereas the initial situation in chapter 2 is unclouded by sin, chapter 4 implies there is something wrong with Cain

---

3. See Wenham, *Genesis 1–15*, 99.

in that his sacrifice is rejected.[4] Eve has to be persuaded by the serpent to disregard God's injunction, but Cain rejects God's appeal to do the right thing (3:2–5//4:6). Whereas Adam gives a truthful reply to God's "Where are you?" Cain responds with a lie ("I do not know") and a joke about shepherds ("Am I my brother's shepherd?") when God asks him about Abel's whereabouts (3:9//4:9). Finally, when God sentences Adam and Eve, they quietly accept it, but Cain protests long and loud: "Cain said to the LORD, 'My punishment is greater than I can bear. Behold, you have driven me today away from the ground, and from your face I shall be hidden. I shall be a fugitive and a wanderer on the earth, and whoever finds me will kill me'" (4:13–14).

Set alongside each other Genesis 3 and 4 tell of a process of degeneration. Through Adam's sin access to the Garden of Eden is forfeit. Through Cain's murder of his brother open violence breaks out in creation. This theme is continued in the short genealogy of Cain's descendants, where Lamech, the first bigamist, boasts of his determination to outdo the violence of his forefather Cain.

> Lamech said to his wives:
> "Adah and Zillah, hear my voice;
> you wives of Lamech, listen to what I say:
> I have killed a man for wounding me,
>> a young man for striking me.
> If Cain's revenge is sevenfold,
>> then Lamech's is seventy-sevenfold."
> (Gen 4:23–24)

Violence thus links the material in the section of Genesis headed by the title, "This is the history of the heavens and the earth when they were created." Human violence later prompts the flood and is a major consideration in the post-flood settlement. We should note that Genesis 1–11 portrays sin and violence getting progressively worse down the generations, in much the same way as books like Judges and Kings do. It portrays sin as endemic, something inherent in the human psyche. This declension in human history sets the grand narrative of Genesis in opposition to the Mesopotamian belief in progress.

---

4. For possible reasons for the rejection of Cain's sacrifice see Wenham, *Genesis 1–15*, 104.

Reading Genesis 1 we argued that it is in dialogue with ancient Near Eastern views of creation: it shares certain assumptions about the divine's involvement in the process, but at the same time it rejects others, including polytheism and the idea that man is an afterthought in the creation schedule. We have noted that the heading in 2:4—"This is the history of the heavens and the earth"—signals very clearly the distinction between the first chapter of Genesis and the subsequent chapters. The heading links the material in 2:4ff with other sections of Genesis with similar headings and implies that the ancient writer and his readers would have viewed all of Genesis 2–50 as having much the same character generically. Protohistory could be the term that sums up its character best. But 1:1—2:3 lacks any such heading and must be evaluated on its own, as an introduction or overture to the rest of Genesis.

If the material in Genesis 2–50 has a common generic character, can comparison with similar materials from the ancient orient help us pin down its genre more precisely? The best parallels to Genesis 2–11 are the Atrahasis epic and the Sumerian Flood Story.[5]

The Atrahasis epic dates from the early second millennium BC. As noted in the previous chapter, it, like Genesis 2, begins with the creation of mankind, continues with various plagues sent by the gods to limit the growth of the human population, and climaxes with the sending of a flood, which destroyed all humans except Atrahasis and his family. Like Noah they escape by building a boat, which eventually lands on a mountain. When Atrahasis emerges, again like Noah, he offers a sacrifice, which the hungry gods crowd around. There are several more detailed similarities with the Genesis story, which will be discussed in the next chapter. But this is sufficient to show that Genesis 2–9 is retelling a story of primeval times that was familiar in the ancient Near East from about 2000 BC, if not before.

The Sumerian Flood Story is another witness to the antiquity of this account. Unfortunately the text is broken, but its editor thought the gaps could be filled with "a fair degree of confidence."[6] If this is correct, the general similarity between this flood story and Genesis 2–9 is clear.

---

5. The Sumerian King List also has more remote parallels see chapter 4.
6. Jacobsen, "Eridu Genesis," 131.

Line 1–36 (lost)	Creation of man and animals, but no irrigation canals, no clothes, no danger from wild animals.	Gen 2–3
37–50	Nintur's (mother goddess) plan to end man's nomadic life.	Gen 4:1–16
51–85 (lost)	Failure of Nintur's plan. Institution of kingship.	
86–100	First cities built including Eridu. Establishment of worship.	Gen 4:17–18 Gen 4:26
101–34 (lost)	List of antediluvian kings. Man's noise.	Gen 5 Gen 6:1–8
135–260	The flood.	Gen 6:9—9:29

Not all the reconstructed content is certain: for some of the more dubious points see my *Genesis 1–15*.[7]

The sequence of topics in the Sumerian Flood Story is quite similar to that in Genesis, i.e., creation, nakedness, nomadism, city building, first worship, human behavior prompting a flood. But the spin put on some of them is quite different. Man's original state is far from paradisial according to the Sumerian view. Rather, it was miserable and pathetic. Nomadism is viewed by both texts as undesirable; but according to Genesis it was the punishment for Cain's sin, whereas the Sumerians saw it as intrinsic to creation. In both versions man is to blame for prompting the gods or God to send the flood. The Sumerians probably blamed the population explosion for making such a racket that it disturbed the gods' heavenly repose; Genesis, on the other hand, makes it clear that it was man's *sinfulness* and *propensity for violence* that triggered the flood. These parallels between the two texts clarify their nature. Both trace a sequence of cause and effect linking the earliest times down to the writer's day or close to it. This is akin to history writing. According to Jacobsen

> This arrangement along a line of time as cause and effect is striking, for it is very much the way a historian arranges his data, and since the data here are mythological we may assign both traditions to a new and separate genre as mytho-historical accounts.[8]

7. Wenham, *Genesis 1–15*, xl.
8. Jacobsen, "Eridu Genesis," 140.

Another feature in common noted by Jacobsen is their interest in chronology

> In both we are given precise figures for respectively the length of reigns and the lifespans of the persons listed, and in both traditions the figures given are extraordinarily large. It seems too . . . that in both traditions the underlying concept is that these early men grew exceedingly slowly from child to adult and on into old age.
>
> This interest in numbers is very curious, for it is characteristic of myths and folktales that they are not concerned with time at all.[9]

Folktales and myths are usually set in an indeterminate era, "once upon a time." "Interest in numbers of years belongs . . . to the style of chronicles and historiography." "This chronological list-form combined, as it is here, with simple mythological narrative is truly unique."[10] So Jacobsen surmises that the Sumerian Flood Story's style is based on the King List and its style. It is these features that led Jacobsen to characterize the Sumerian Flood Story and Genesis 1–11 as mythohistorical. As "myth" is a term open to misunderstanding, I prefer to characterize the accounts as protohistorical.

Though Genesis 2–9 and the Sumerian Flood Story have much in common, theologically there are enormous contrasts. There is the clear monotheism of Genesis as opposed to the polytheism of the Sumerian Flood Story. The motive for the flood is quite different too. But what Jacobsen highlights is the different direction of history the two accounts offer.

> Note how decisively these materials have been transformed in the biblical account, altering radically their original meaning and import.
>
> The Eridu Genesis (=Sumerian Flood Story) takes throughout . . . an affirmative and optimistic view of existence; it believes in progress. Things were not nearly as good to begin with as they have become since . . . .
>
> In the biblical account it is the other way around. Things began as perfect from God's hand and grew then steadily worse through man's sinfulness until God finally had to do away with all mankind except for the pious Noah who would beget a new and better stock.

---

9. Ibid., 140–41.
10. Ibid., 141.

> The moral judgment here introduced and the ensuing pessimistic viewpoint could not be more different from the tenor of the Sumerian tale: only the assurance that such a flood will not recur is common to both.[11]

The emphasis on sin in the book of Genesis from chapter 3 onwards is new when compared with chapter 1, but the same unclouded picture is found in chapter 2. We saw that the creation of man is, in chapter 1, the climax of God's creative work, which all the heavenly host are invited to observe and perhaps participate in—that is the implication of the first plural "let *us* make man in *our* image." But God's special care for man is already evident in his creative acts on the other days. Those things that are particularly vital for human life—dry land, plants, the sun and moon—are described most fully. The same emphasis is apparent in chapter 2, which pictures God, having created Adam first of all, looking to see what else he needs. So he makes for Adam a luxuriant garden replete with abundant water supply and a variety of fruit trees. Then come the animals, which it is hoped will relieve his loneliness. But their failure to fulfill Adam's needs prompts God to create Eve. Thus, the whole drift of the story is God's concern for man's welfare. Though the creation of Adam from the dust of the ground brings Genesis closer to one Babylonian tradition that man was created from clay mixed with a god's blood, the general picture is quite different. Whereas *Enuma elish* and the Atrahasis epic see the creation of mankind as an afterthought to spare the gods toil, Genesis not only makes man the climax of creation but describes a Creator intent on meeting all mankind's needs.

It is this positive view of humanity that underlies the first command given to man, "be fruitful and multiply," which is made possible by creating them in two sexes, male and female. In Genesis 1 it is not clear how the creation of man was achieved, nor how many humans God made to start with. *Enuma elish* mentions only one, whereas Atrahasis tells of Enki and Nintu creating seven human couples. Genesis 2, however, envisages just one couple being created, the father and mother of the whole human race. This enables them to function as the archetypes of every man or woman. This allows the writer of Genesis 2 to draw a universal principle from the creation of woman from Adam's rib. "Therefore, a man shall leave his father and his mother and hold fast to his wife, and they shall become one flesh" (Gen 2:24). If, as in the Atrahasis epic, God had created multiple humans,

---

11. Ibid., 142.

this link between the first humans and the later readers would not be so clear.

The creation of just one partner for Adam also has another implication. We have noted how concerned God is that all Adam's needs should be satisfied. So one might ask, why did he not create several Eves for Adam, or even an extra Adam or two? Clearly Genesis presupposes that heterosexual monogamy is best for man from a social point of view and it enables the fulfillment of the command to be fruitful and multiply. It pictures Adam breaking into song, or at least poetry, when God, taking the role of bride's father, introduces her to Adam.

> Then the man said,
> "This at last is bone of my bones and flesh of my flesh;
> she shall be called Woman, because she was taken out of Man."
> (Gen 2:23)

The comments "bone of my bones" and "flesh of my flesh" may appear to be merely a reflection on the story of the creation of Eve, but these phrases are used elsewhere to describe blood relationships between family members. So here these phrases underline the intimate connection between spouses in marriage. This is not a concern of the Atrahasis epic, which sees the creation of human couples as a model of the midwife's role.

Another contrast between Babylonian tradition and Genesis 1 concerns food. Whereas the former held that man was created to produce food for the gods, Genesis declares sees things very differently—God provides man and beast with food. But only plants and fruit trees, not animals. Genesis 1 pictures an originally vegetarian world. The same seems to be implied in Eden. "And out of the ground the LORD God made to spring up every tree that is pleasant to the sight and good for food" (Gen 2:9). There is no hint that the animals were to be killed for meat: rather they were intended to be a help and companions for man. The world was intended to be a peaceful place with all God's creatures living in harmony with each other. In the previous chapter we saw that the goal of creation was the Sabbath, the day God rested from his labors. In ancient thought the gods rested in a temple when one was dedicated to them, and we argued that Genesis views the creation of the world as creating a temple for God to dwell in. Peace between all God's creatures and his presence on earth is the essence of the divine scheme.

The same idea is expressed even more clearly in Genesis 2. Temples in ancient times were supposed to be built on top of the cosmic mountain, a notion fully developed in Morales, *The Tabernacle Pre-figured: Cosmic Mountain Ideology in Genesis and Exodus*. This cosmic mountain had its top in heaven and its base in the underworld. It was the centre of the world. It was the source of water and fertility and the dwelling place of the gods. The Garden of Eden has some obvious similarities to this idea of a cosmic mountain. God was present there in a special way, for he used to walk in the garden in the cool of the day. It was the source of abundant water, for a river flowed out of Eden and became four great streams, three of which are well known, Gihon, which rises in Jerusalem, the Tigris, and the Euphrates. It is not immediately obvious from Genesis that Eden was on a mountain, but this is mentioned in Ezekiel 28 where the king of Tyre is said to have been placed in Eden on the mountain of God, from where he was later ejected because of his sin (Ezek 28:13–16). In identifying the imagery of the cosmic mountain as built into Genesis 2–3 we underline the point that Eden is pre-eminently the place where God dwells. In so far as Adam and Eve represent the whole human race, not just Israel,[12] we can see Eden as the place where God dwelt with mankind.

This point is made by another aspect of Eden imagery: many of its features anticipate the design of the tabernacle and the temple in Jerusalem. For example, both sanctuaries had their main entrances facing the east. This is implied by the stationing of the cherubim with the flaming sword on this side of the garden. These cherubim were the traditional guardians of holy places (3:24). Furthermore, tabernacle and temple were adorned with cherubim over the ark and woven into the curtains. Gold and precious stones were also part of the decoration of these sanctuaries and were also found in Eden (2:12). Water flowed out of the temple, according to Ezekiel 47:1–12 (cf. Gen 2:10–14). The seven-branched candlestick or *menorah* is described in tree-like terms in Exodus 25:31–40; 37:17–24, and corresponds to the tree of life in the garden.[13] We have already noted that God walked in the garden in the cool of the day. The same verb, "walk" (*hithallēk*), describes God's presence in the tabernacle in Leviticus 26:12 and 2 Samuel 7:6. Finally Adam was put in the garden "to work it and keep it" (2:15), a combination of verbs used to describe the work of the Levites in the tabernacle according to Numbers 3:7–8; 8:26; 18:5–6. Through this

---

12. Pace Postell, *Adam as Israel*.
13. Meyers, *Tabernacle Menorah*.

comparison the garden is portrayed as the archetypal sanctuary, where God and man should dwell together in harmony. And Adam is the archetypal priest of this primeval temple.

This harmony is shattered by the couple's disregard for God's instructions. His warning was quite clear: "You may surely eat of every tree of the garden, but of the tree of the knowledge of good and evil you shall not eat, for in the day that you eat of it you shall surely die" (Gen 2:16–17). But, of course, they did eat the forbidden fruit, and Genesis 3 spells out the consequences. The story is well known to Bible readers, but unusually for this part of Scripture, there are no good oriental parallels. A fall story is, of course, hard to fit into a philosophy of progress, which Jacobsen has argued is integral to the Sumerian Flood Story.

A possible, but rather unclear parallel is found in the Adapa traditions.[14] Adapa is one of the seven *apkallu*s, sages who rose from the sea to teach mankind the arts of civilization. Whether he was the first or last of the sages is disputed, but he is certainly the best known. The myth begins by mentioning his role as priest in Ea's temple at Eridu, where he offered sacrifice every day. He also went fishing to feed Ea. By cursing the South Wind and thereby breaking its wing, Adapa offended the gods and was summoned to heaven. Ea warned Adapa not to drink the water or eat the food that would be offered in heaven or he would die. Adapa duly follows this advice and is laughed at by the god Anu, who lived in heaven, because the water and food would have given him immortality. So Adapa returns to earth and is banished to the Apsu, the fresh-water-ocean home of Ea.

This tale has certain resemblances to Genesis 2–3. First, the name Adapa sounds like Adam. Second, Adapa serves as priest in Ea's temple. We have noted that Eden is described in terms that foreshadow the later tabernacle and temples in Jerusalem, and that Adam is commissioned "to work and keep" the garden, phrases that anticipate the role of Levites in the tabernacle. Third, Ea's injunction to Adapa not to eat or drink the heavenly bread and water parallels God's ban on eating from the tree of knowledge. But the rest of the tale is rather different. Adapa obeys his god, whereas Adam does not. By not eating, Adapa forfeits his chance of immortality, whereas by eating Adam loses that chance. Whereas the Adapa tale challenges the value of obeying one's deity, Genesis endorses it. If Genesis knows the Adapa myth, it is rewriting it to present a new theology and

---

14. For a survey of these traditions and their possible interpretations see Lowery, *Toward a Poetics*, 214–26.

ethic. The God of Genesis does not deceive his worshippers, as the Adapa myth implies Ea did, and as the Serpent claims the God of Genesis did, and so his commands must be obeyed to the letter.

In Babylonian tradition Adapa appeared at the same time as the first king, and it was with the establishment of kingship—it is said to have been let down from heaven—that the first significant steps were taken to organize mankind. So Adapa is associated with the first generation of humanity. He was a Mesopotamian Everyman. His fate represented the fate of every human being and therefore had a universal validity. "In other words, the significance of the Adapa story to its audience would have been primarily archetypal, as the Genesis accounts would possibly have been for its audience."[15]

I would be more confident than Lowery about Genesis 2–3. It is archetypal or paradigmatic: it shows what happens every time someone sins. Sin is disobeying God's law: here "you shall not eat." And disobeying God's law has both spiritual and physical consequences. The spiritual consequence is alienation from God. Adam and Eve first hide among the trees and then are expelled from the garden. As the garden, the cosmic mountain, is the source of life, expulsion is a death sentence: "in the day that you eat of it you shall surely die" (Gen 2:17). The physical consequences may take longer to appear, but they embrace all areas of human existence, from pain in childbirth to daily toil to physical death. Unchecked sin manifests itself in evermore-serious ways with evermore-serious consequences, as the story of Cain and his descendants illustrates.

This picture of sin and its effects is presupposed in the rest of Scripture. The history of Israel as told in the Old Testament shows this repeatedly. Transgression of the covenant, especially idolatry, led to the nation suffering, most frequently by foreign invasion, but ultimately by their exile from the land. The land of Canaan is described in Deuteronomy in Edenic terms. It is a land flowing with milk and honey.

> But the land that you are going over to possess is a land of hills and valleys, which drinks water by the rain from heaven, a land that the LORD your God cares for. The eyes of the LORD your God are always upon it, from the beginning of the year to the end of the year.
>
> (Deut 11:11–12)

---

15. Lowery, *Toward a Poetics*, 224.

Rethinking Genesis 2-4

It is Israel's privilege to have been given the law.

> For what great nation is there that has a god so near to it as the LORD our God is to us, whenever we call upon him? And what great nation is there, that has statutes and rules so righteous as all this law that I set before you today?
> (Deut 4:7–8)

It is therefore Israel's duty to keep the law, and most of Deuteronomy is taken up with exhortation to obey it. The positive incentive is that so doing will ensure that the land will indeed become Israel's. But positive urgings are laced with negative warnings about the consequences of disobedience: drought, crop failure, disease, children dying, defeat in war, and ultimately exile from the land. Although Deuteronomy urges obedience, it envisages that compliance will not be forthcoming. And that is the story of the histories from the book of Judges onwards. They trace a progressive decline in royal and national adherence to the law, which culminates in the sack of Jerusalem in 587 BC. It is not just Israel's history tellers who in retrospect trace national degeneration, but the prophets warned their contemporaries in advance of the likely outcome of the neglect of the law. A similar message is inculcated by the books of Proverbs and the Psalms. The Psalms have some very somber assessments. The psalm most completely duplicated in the Psalter, Psalm 14, contains the lines:

> The LORD looks down from heaven on the children of man,
> > to see if there are any who understand,
> > who seek after God.
> They have all turned aside; together they have become corrupt;
> > there is none who does good,
> > not even one.
> (Ps 14:2–3 = 53:2–3)

While Psalm 143 says:

> Enter not into judgment with your servant,
> > for no one living is righteous before you.
> (Ps 143:2)

This emphasis on the universality, indeed inevitability of human sin, is inherent in the Genesis account of the fall. It offers not just an analysis of what constitutes sin and of what its effects are, but because Adam and

Eve represent every man and woman, it teaches that Everyman is a sinner, liable to judgment, and in need of divine grace to save him or her from sin's clutches. In this sense, these chapters are paradigmatic, in that they explain through a story what sin is and what it costs the human race.

But is it *just* this—a fable, a just-so story, or even a myth? It is easy to jump to such a conclusion, but these labels hardly do justice to the centrality of these ideas to biblical theology. We have already noted that the title of this section (2:4—4:26) of Genesis ("These are the generations of . . .") links it to subsequent sections of the book (e.g., 6:9; 11:27; 37:2). This implies we should see Adam and Eve in the same light as the patriarchs, Abraham, Jacob and Esau, and so on. A similar conclusion might be drawn from the genealogies, which link Adam to Noah in ten generations and Noah to Abraham in another ten generations. Features of the fall narrative point in a similar direction. The curse on the snake that condemns him to crawl on his belly is not a recurring discovery of Everyman, but something taken for granted. Pain, toil, and death are not new every time someone sins: rather they are part of the human inheritance. So too is life outside the garden: no one starts life in the garden and then gets expelled today. It is portrayed as a one-off event, so that Cain does not sin within the garden but outside it. These features point to the fall as a unique event, not merely a paradigmatic one. Jacobsen in his discussion of the Sumerian Flood Story pointed to various features that made it like history.

> In the "Eridu Genesis" moreover the progression is clearly a logical one of cause and effect: the wretched state of natural man touches the motherly heart of Nintur, who has him improve his lot by settling down in cities and building temples; and she gives him a king to lead and organise. As this chain of cause and effect leads from nature to civilization, so a following such chain carries from the early cities and kings over into the story of the flood. . . . Now this arrangement along a line of time as cause and effect is striking, for it is very much the way a historian arranges his data, and since the data here are mythological we may assign both traditions to a new and separate genre as mytho-historical accounts.[16]

The Sumerian Flood Story's interest in chronology also gives it a historical feel, which Jacobsen argues adds further weight to his description of it as mytho-historical.[17] Cause and effect as well as an interest in

---

16. Jacobsen, "Eridu Genesis," 140.
17. Ibid., 141.

chronology also characterize the opening chapters of Genesis, particularly in the genealogies and flood story. So this might tempt some to adopt Jacobsen's generic category of mytho-historical, but the way Genesis links Adam to his descendants through narratives and genealogy make me think, as I've previously mentioned, that *protohistorical* describes this material in a way more congruent with the author's own understanding.

Summary

To sum up: with chapter 2 verse 4 the narrative of Genesis takes off. 1:1—2:3 is essentially an overture to the book, but with 2:4 we have the first of ten titles to major sections of Genesis. The form of the title ("These are the generations of . . ."/"This is the history of . . .") intimates that the story of Adam and Eve is comparable to the stories of Abraham, Isaac, and Jacob, whose biographies have a similar heading. A similar point is made by linking the genealogies of the antediluvian patriarchs with the later patriarchs, who lived after the flood.

But chapters 2 to 4 also look back to Genesis 1. A theology first proclaimed in chapter 1 is elaborated in chapters 2–4. Genesis 1 announced an original monotheism where the one God reigned supreme, instead of a pantheon of rival gods and goddesses. The sovereign power of this Creator God is demonstrated by his word calling into being all things necessary for human flourishing in the first five days and then creating man on the sixth day. This contrasts with ancient oriental views of man's creation, which see it as a way of providing food for the gods, whereas Genesis 1 describes a God whose concern is man's welfare.

Genesis 2 reinforces this picture of the primacy of God's concern for mankind. The creation of Adam from the dust of the earth is followed by God planting a garden full of fruit trees to satisfy his appetite and the creation of animals as potential companions. When this does not meet Adam's needs, Eve is created from his rib, thereby making it possible for them to be fruitful and multiply. In this way, the ideals of chapter 1 are enhanced and clarified.

That chapter concluded with God resting on the seventh day, suggesting that the creation of the cosmos was seen as building a temple in which God could dwell. This picture is developed in chapter 2's description of the Garden of Eden in terms later used of the tabernacle and temple. The garden is planted on the cosmic mountain and is portrayed as God's earthly dwelling place where God and man should live together in harmony.

But this harmony is shattered by Adam and Eve's eating of the forbidden fruit and consequently being expelled from the garden, a pattern replicated by Abel's murder at his brother's hand. This doctrine of the fall introduces a radically new note to the primeval history. While oriental theology believed in progress, that human society was evolving towards a higher civilization, Genesis affirms the opposite. Society disintegrates without divine intervention. The biblical writers spell this out in poetry and prose in many parts of the Old Testament, but nowhere so clearly as in the flood story, which is the topic of the next chapter.

3

Rethinking Genesis 6–9

Creation Destroyed and Restored

Introduction

IN THE PREVIOUS CHAPTERS we have argued that Genesis 1 is an overture to the book, which provides the reader with the ideological spectacles to read the following chapters empathetically. With chapter 2 the grand narrative of Scripture begins. It reaffirms some of the key ideas of chapter 1, such as the role of man and the divine design for a world in which God and man live together in harmony. Chapters 3 and 4 describe the world as it is, alienated from God and riven with strife between man and beast, man and wife, man and nature. This violent situation gets even worse in chapter 4 with the first murder and Lamech threatening seventy-sevenfold vengeance on anyone who assaults him. This forms the backdrop to the longest narrative in early Genesis, which tells of Noah and the flood (Genesis 6–9). But the flood story is more than the paradigm of divine judgment; it is a tale of de-creation and re-creation.[1] Not only do the plants and animals emerge from the waters in a way that echoes the days of creation, but Noah is a second-Adam figure from whom the whole human race is descended. Through this narrative Genesis' understanding of creation and fall are clarified and nuanced. As in our previous chapters we shall proceed by analyzing the structure of this narrative and its parallels with other ancient flood stories.

---

1. Blenkinsopp, *Creation, Un-creation, Re-creation*.

In this way we shall hope to refine our characterization of the genres of Genesis 1–11.

The Structure of Genesis 6–9

We noted earlier that Genesis is divided into a prologue (1:1—2:3) and ten major sections each headed by the title, "This is the history of . . ." (or "These are the generations of . . ."). One of these headings is found in 6:9, "This is the history of Noah," thereby marking the beginning of the flood story. The next heading is 10:1, "This is the history of the sons of Noah," which implies the flood story ends in 9:29. Furthermore both titles are preceded by a trailer that announces the topic of the following narrative. 6:5–8 obviously predicts the flood and summarizes why it is coming and why Noah will escape.

> The LORD saw that the wickedness of man was great in the earth, and that every intention of the thoughts of his heart was only evil continually. And the LORD regretted that he had made man on the earth, and it grieved him to his heart. So the LORD said, "I will blot out man whom I have created from the face of the land, man and animals and creeping things and birds of the heavens, for I am sorry that I have made them." But Noah found favor in the eyes of the LORD.
> (Gen 6:5–8)

The trailer before 10:1 is not so immediately obvious. Chapter 10 is the Table of the Nations, setting out how the nations of the world relate to each other and to Israel. The table declares that these nations fall into three groups, each of which is constituted by being descended from one of Noah's three sons—Shem, Ham, and Japhet. The northernmost peoples are descended from Japhet (10:2–5). From Ham are traced many of Israel's enemies, including Egypt, Babylon, the Philistines, and the Canaanites (10:6–20). From Shem descended various eastern tribes and, of course, Israel (10:21–31).

The trailer to the Table of the Nations is the episode in 9:20–27 in which Ham treats Noah disrespectfully[2] and is cursed for it. Shem and

---

2. The nature of Ham's offence is unclear. See Wenham, *Genesis 1–15*, 198–202. Also Gagnon, *Bible and Homosexual Practice*, 63–71. I would now favour homosexual incest as more likely than its alternatives. These sins are often attributed to the Canaanites in the OT (see Lev 18).

Rethinking Genesis 6–9

Japhet try to atone for their brother's behavior and are blessed for so doing. This curse and blessing determined the fate of their descendants. Noah pronounced a curse on Ham's son Canaan.

> Cursed be Canaan;
> a servant of servants shall he be to his brothers.
> (Gen 9:25)

Ham's descendants, especially Canaan, were among those later conquered by Israel (see 10:15–19). Conversely, Shem and Japhet are assured:

> Blessed be the LORD, the God of Shem;
> and let Canaan be his servant.
> May God enlarge Japheth,
> and let him dwell in the tents of Shem,
> and let Canaan be his servant.
> (Gen 9:26–27)

It may seem curious to us to have a tale of incest tacked on to the flood story, but we should note that the other tale of universal judgment in Genesis, the destruction of Sodom and Gomorrah, also ends with a story of incest with the righteous hero (19:30–38) and, like 9:18–27, explains the origin of some of Israel's neighbors. We shall reflect on the theological significance of these codas later, but first note some of the similarities between these final episodes. Both occur after stories in which all the wicked are destroyed leaving just one righteous man and his family to survive. In both tales the righteous hero gets drunk—Noah apparently because he was not aware of wine's potential and Lot because his daughters persuaded him to drink too much, so that they could have intercourse with him. It seems most likely that Ham treated his father similarly, lusting after him—or even engaging in homosexual incest with him. Both stories insist that the righteous hero was asleep when he was assaulted by his offspring, and both connect the origin of some of Israel's most persistent enemies with these episodes. Moab and Ammon were descended from Lot, and the Canaanites were one of the many enemies of Israel descended from Noah through his son Ham.

These narratives and genealogies help us to define the nature of the materials in Genesis 1–11. However, the main concern of my chapter here is to determine the relationship between the accounts of creation and fall in chapters 1 to 4 and the flood story in chapters 6 to 9. This, I hope, will shed light on the ancient understanding of these events and the accounts of them. We begin as before by looking at the literary features of the flood story. Relying on 6:9 ("This is the history of Noah"/"These are the generations of Noah") as a marker of a new section, we see that the rest of the flood story down to 9:19 forms a long and complex palistrophe,[3] probably the most detailed in the whole Bible.

---

3. Palistrophe is a structure that turns back (Greek *palin* "backwards" *strophe* "turning"). For a fuller analysis of the structure, see Wenham, "Coherence" and "Method."

Rethinking Genesis 6-9

A Noah (6:10a)
  B Shem, Ham, and Japhet (10b)
    C Ark to be built (14-16)
      D Flood announced (17)
        E Covenant with Noah (18-20)
          F Food in the ark (21)
            G Command to enter ark (7:1-3)
              H Seven days waiting for the flood (4-5)
                I Seven days waiting for the flood (7-10)
                  J Entry to ark (11-15)
                    K Yahweh shuts Noah in (16)
                      L Forty days flood (17a)
                        M Waters increase (17b-18)
                          N Mountains covered (19-20)
                            O 150 days waters prevail (21-24)
                              P GOD REMEMBERS NOAH (8:1)
                            O" 150 days waters abate (3)
                          N" Mountain tops visible (4-5)
                        M" Waters abate (5)
                      L" Forty days end (6a)
                    K" Noah opens ark window (6b)
                  J" Birds leave ark (7-9)
                I" Seven days waiting for water to subside (10-11)
              H" Seven days waiting for water to subside (12-13)
            G" Command to leave ark (15-17)
          F" Food outside ark (9:1-4)
        E" Covenant with all flesh (8-10)
      D" No flood in future (11-17)
    C" Ark (18a)
  B" Shem, Ham and Japhet (18b)
A" Noah (19)

Palistrophes like this are quite a frequent device in the Old Testament, especially in the two-member form AB-BA, which is usually called a chiasmus (from the Greek letter Chi (χ). In one perspective the use of a palistrophe to tell the flood story is not surprising. The way in which it tells the story mirrors the sequence of events. The people embark on the ark and later disembark. The waters rise and then fall again. The mountains are covered with water but eventually reappear. If these were the only correspondences, we might dismiss them as coincidence. But some of them are so contrived that they must be deliberate. The days mentioned have been arranged artificially to fit the palistrophic structure.

H Seven days waiting for the flood (4–5)
  I Seven days waiting for the flood (7–10)
    L Forty days flood (17a)
      O 150 days waters prevail (21–24)
        P GOD REMEMBERS NOAH (8:1)
      O" 150 days waters abate (3)
    L" Forty days end (6a)
  I" Seven days waiting for water to subside (10–11)
H" Seven days waiting for water to subside (12–13)

Note how the numbers in the first half of the palistrophe (HILO) are reversed in the second (O"L"I"H"). But this is contrived because the first two mentions of seven days actually refer to just one week, the week between the command to enter the ark and the flood's onset. Whereas the last two mentions of seven days cover the three weeks of the dove's reconnaissance flights. This molding of the chronological data demonstrates that the writer wants to do more than merely tell a story: he is anxious to make a point. The most obvious concerns the mid-point of the account. "But God remembered Noah" (8:1). It is God who saved Noah, not, as in other oriental accounts, the hero's own energy and good fortune.

This palistrophe falls into two halves: the first tells of the destruction of the first creation, while the second describes a new creation emerging from the waters and the ark. We could describe it as de-creation and re-creation. De-creation culminates in the world being once again submerged in water as in Genesis 1:2, "The earth was without form and void, and darkness was over the face of the deep. And the Spirit of God was hovering over the face of the waters." It is not only in the general picture of the world reverting to a watery ocean that makes this text echo Genesis 1. Both emphasize the variety of species affected:

> And God said, "Let the earth bring forth living creatures according to their kinds—livestock and creeping things and beasts of the earth according to their kinds." And it was so.
> (Gen 1:24)

> On the very same day Noah and his sons, Shem and Ham and Japheth, and Noah's wife and the three wives of his sons with them entered the ark, they and every beast, according to its kind, and all the livestock according to their kinds, and every creeping thing that creeps on the earth, according to its kind, and every bird, according to its kind, every winged creature.
> (7:13–14)

The passage continues using terms from both chapters 1 and 2 of Genesis, "male and female" (1:27) and "breath of life" (2:7. Cf. 7:15–16).

Echoes of the creation are even more obvious in the second half of the palistrophe, which describes the re-creation of the earth. The heavens, of course, were not destroyed in the flood, so there is no mention of light, the firmament, and the heavenly bodies being recreated. Similarly the fish were not destroyed in the flood, so there is no mention of the earth being restocked with them.

But immediately after saying "God remembered Noah" "God made a wind to blow over the earth" (8:1), which recalls "The Spirit/wind of God was hovering over the face of the deep" (1:2). God's wind makes the water subside (8:1) so that the dry land appears (cf. 1:9). According to Genesis 1, the third day saw not only the emergence of dry land, but also the growth of plants and trees. But in Genesis 8 it takes at least 150 days for the waters to abate (8:3) and more than seven months for the earth to dry out[4] (8:4, 14). It was during this period that the dove was sent out and came back with "a freshly picked olive leaf," demonstrating the re-creation of plants and trees (8:11).

---

4. Note two different terms are used for drying out in 8:13 and 14. It is the second, *yābēš*, that matches the term for dry land in Genesis 1:9–10 *yabbāšāh*.

In Genesis 1 birds were created on the fifth day and man and other animals on the sixth day. They emerge together from the ark to repopulate the earth a year and ten days after the onset of the flood (1:20–27; 8:14–19). Birds were originally told to be fruitful and multiply on the fifth day and mankind was given the same instruction on the sixth (1:22, 28). All creatures that survived the flood are given this injunction in 8:17. An allusion to the fall and its consequences is found in 8:21, "I will never again curse the ground because of man" (cf. 3:17). Genesis 9:1–7 addresses the vegetarian diet prescribed for all creatures in 1:29–30.

> And God said, "Behold, I have given you every plant yielding seed that is on the face of all the earth, and every tree with seed in its fruit. You shall have them for food. And to every beast of the earth and to every bird of the heavens and to everything that creeps on the earth, everything that has the breath of life, I have given every green plant for food."

This rule is abrogated in 9:3–4 and replaced by a simple ban on the consumption of blood. "Every moving thing that lives shall be food for you. And as I gave you the green plants, I give you everything. But you shall not eat flesh with its life, that is, its blood."

One final link between the old and new creation is seen in the law on homicide. Genesis 1:27 mentions that man is made in God's image, but this is associated with man's rule over the rest of creation. The divine image makes every human being a representative of God and therefore he or she is expected to manage the rest of creation in a godlike manner. But unfortunately this has not always been the case. Since Genesis 1 much blood has been shed, which is an assault on God's representatives. The wave of violence eventually prompted God to send the flood (6:11, 13). To protect God's image-bearers and forestall another catastrophic judgment Genesis 9:5–6 ordains:

> For your lifeblood I will require a reckoning: from every beast I will require it and from man. From his fellow man I will require a reckoning for the life of man.
> Whoever sheds the blood of man,
> by man shall his blood be shed,
> for God made man in his own image.

These multiple quotations from and allusions to Genesis 1–3 show that the flood story may be read as a kind of commentary on the preceding chapters. They invite us to compare the account of the new creation with that of the first creation. The accounts share the same starting point: the Spirit or wind of God moving over the primeval ocean that covered the hidden landmass. The parallels continue with the ebbing of the waters, which discloses the dry land. Whereas Genesis 1 could be read as achieving this in a single day, it takes several months in Genesis 8. With the emergence of dry land vegetation appears: in the first account all sorts of plants and fruit trees are seen, but only an olive leaf in the second. Finally, all the land-based creatures are created or come out of the ark.

But there are several notable differences between the two creations. We have already noted that certain zones, such as the heavens and the sea, were unaffected by the flood, so that no new work of creation was required in them. And there are not only omissions, but changes. The cause of the flood was violence affecting all flesh, which probably includes animals as well as humans. This colors the re-creation picture. The first creation account ended with the observation, "And God saw everything that he had made, and behold, it was very good," before reporting that God rested on the seventh day. The second account ends more circumspectly, with the promise that there would never be another flood that would be so destructive. This rather implies that another great flood might be warranted, but divine forbearance would lead it to be averted. "When I bring clouds over the earth and the bow is seen in the clouds, I will remember my covenant that is between me and you and every living creature of all flesh. And the waters shall never again become a flood to destroy all flesh" (Gen 9:14–15).

The Chronology of the Flood

However, the most striking difference between the two accounts is in their chronology. The first creation takes a bare six days, whereas the re-creation after the flood takes more than half a year. It is characteristic of the flood narrative to date precisely the various phases of destruction and restoration. There are in fact two ways the events are dated: first, by noting how many days elapsed for something to occur. E.g., 150 days for the waters to abate (8:3). These time lapses form part of the palistrophe that we have already mentioned (see above). The second way is dating events by Noah's age on that day, e.g., the flood started on the seventeenth day of the second month in Noah's 600th year, while Noah left the ark on the twenty-seventh day of the second month of Noah's 601st year. This detailed chronology of the flood and its aftermath is unique in Genesis. Other events may be dated by the age of the hero at the time (e.g., Abraham was a hundred at Isaac's birth, 21:5), but not by the day or month. Why does the flood story offer such precision? There is no obvious answer, but if we merge the two methods of timing as they are found in our present text, a possible answer is found.

Date in Noah's Life (dd.mm.yr)	Period	Day of the Week
(10.2.600)	After seven days flood came (7:10)	Sunday flood announced
17.2.600	*Rain and flood began (7:11)*	*Sunday*
(27.3.600)	Forty days and nights rain (7:12)	Friday rain ended
	Forty days flood on earth (7:17)	
	150 days waters strong (7:24)	
(15.7.600)	After 150 days waters abate (8:3)	Wednesday
17.7.600	*Ark rests on Ararat (8:4)*	*Friday*
1.10.600	*Mountain tops seen (8:5)*	*Wednesday*
(10.11.600)	End of forty days raven sent out (8:6–7)	Sunday
(24.11.600)	Another seven days dove's second flight (8:10)	Sunday
(1.12.600)	Another seven days dove's third flight (8:12)	Sunday
1.1.601	*Waters dried up (8:13)*	*Wednesday*
27.2.601	*Earth dry. Exit from ark (8:14)*	*Wednesday*

This table dates different stages in the flood event. The first two columns are taken direct from Genesis. The italic entries simply sum up the text as it stands. The plain entries in the middle column again simply repeat the textual data, and the dates in the first column have been calculated on the basis of the time periods in the middle column.[5]

---

5. To fit all the time spans of forty and 150 days into the chronology of Noah's life requires the assumption that some of the figures have been duplicated, perhaps to enhance the palistrophe. For further discussion, see Wenham, "Coherence," 442–45.

But the most interesting conclusions may be drawn from the third column. How can one know the day of the week on which different events occurred? This is where the issue becomes somewhat speculative. If we assume Genesis used the calendar used in the book of Jubilees, a second-century BC document, the events took place on known days of the week.[6] The rain and floods according to this calendar began on Sunday, which is the first day of the week, the first day of creation according to Genesis 1. They continued for forty days till Friday (Gen 7:12). In other words, the destructive phase of the flood began on Sunday and ended on a Friday, just as the original creation began on a Sunday and ended on Friday, the day before the Sabbath. In this way, de-creation mirrors creation chronologically as well as substantially, but it took a bit longer, forty days instead of six.

Other dates seem to highlight the importance of the Sabbath. God announces the flood on a Sunday, the first day of the working week, and then it starts on the next Sunday. The righteous Noah also seems to observe the Sabbath. At least, when sending out the raven and dove, he always does it at weekly intervals and sends out the birds on Sunday. Finally, the ark grounds on the Mountains of Ararat on a Friday. Is this because that prevents it travelling on yet another Sabbath? Whatever one thinks about the use of the Jubilees calendar, it is clear that like Genesis 1 the flood narrative is underlining the importance of the Sabbath. God observes the Sabbath and so does righteous Noah. This suggests that commending Sabbath observance is more the function of the chronology than recording the exact length of the process of de-creation and re-creation. If destroying creation took forty days and recreating the earth took more than six months, it would seem unlikely that the days of Genesis 1 or the days and months in Genesis 7–8 are understood strictly chronologically. Rather they encourage observance of the Sabbath.

The flood story is not just concerned about the Sabbath, its central concern is human sin, which it traces to the heart of man. "The LORD saw that the wickedness of man was great in the earth, and that every intention of the thoughts of his heart was only evil continually" (Gen 6:5). The wicked heart leads to corrupt behavior, especially violence: "Now the earth was corrupt in God's sight, and the earth was filled with violence. And God saw the earth, and behold, it was corrupt, for all flesh had corrupted their way on the earth" (Gen 6:11–12). These introductory comments explain the reason for the flood. The universality of sin ("all flesh") and its

---

6. See Jaubert, *La date*, 33–35.

deepseatedness ("every intention of the thoughts of his heart") necessitate the destruction of the old order and a new start with the one blameless and righteous person in his generation. So one might hope that when Noah and the animals emerge from the ark all would be well, and sin and violence a thing of the past. But almost immediately we realize this is not so. Noah offers a series of burnt offerings of clean animals on which Genesis comments as follows: "And when the LORD smelled the pleasing aroma, the LORD said in his heart, 'I will never again curse the ground because of man, for the intention of man's heart is evil from his youth. Neither will I ever again strike down every living creature as I have done'" (Gen 8:21).

"For the intention of man's heart is evil from his youth" implies that the problem of the human heart has not been eradicated. It is purely God's mercy, prompted by the sacrifices, that ensures that the earth will not suffer another catastrophic flood.

But if the human heart is still evil, does that mean violence could again become a problem? Will the offspring of Lamech still wreak seventy-sevenfold vengeance? The text sees this as likely and prescribes limited retribution to keep future Lamechs in check

> Whoever sheds the blood of man,
> by man shall his blood be shed,
> for God made man in his own image.
> (Gen 9:6)

With this decree, the talion principle is introduced—the principle that punishment should fit the crime and be proportionate to the offence. It is better known as the "eye-for-eye" principle, often caricatured as vicious, because it is assumed to require that the threat of mutilation was intended to be taken literally. This was not the case. Often damages could be paid instead (see Exod 21:28–36). Here we cannot expound it further:[7] it is sufficient to note that Genesis assumes that violence, like the corrupt heart, will be an ongoing problem. This point is proved by the final episode in the history of Noah in which he overindulges in wine, thereby shaming himself and prompting Ham's evil heart to show itself. Noah's misbehavior may be seen to parallel Adam's fall, which also involved consumption of forbidden fruit and a worse offence by his son. In this way, the flood narrative underlines the sinful nature of mankind, which was first apparent in the fall.

---

7. See further, Burnside, *God, Justice and Society*, 275–83.

Babylonian Parallels

We have characterized Genesis 6–9 as a commentary on Genesis 1–4 because it underlines and clarifies the message of the book's opening chapters. It may also be described as a commentary on earlier ancient Near Eastern flood stories, though as we shall see, it really involves a drastic rewriting of the older versions. The Assyrian version of the flood story was in fact the first detailed parallel to the stories of Genesis to come to light. It was deciphered and translated by George Adam Smith from tablets discovered in Ashurbanipal's palace at Nineveh and published in 1872. It forms part of the Gilgamesh epic, the longest Babylonian poem known to date. The epic tells of the efforts of Gilgamesh, the king of Uruk, to acquire immortality. Eventually he meets Utnapishtim, otherwise known as Atrahasis, the only human to have achieved eternal life. From Atrahasis Gilgamesh learns the story of the flood and how he survived. Gilgamesh is given a plant that can endow its owner with eternal youth, but it is swallowed by a snake, thus frustrating Gilgamesh's hope of immortality. It is widely held that the flood story in the Gilgamesh epic has been borrowed from the Atrahasis epic, which we discussed earlier.[8] We noted then how the structure of the Atrahasis epic was comparable to that of Genesis in that it began with the creation of man and ended with the flood. But though the flood story fits more securely into the Atrahasis epic, we shall use the Gilgamesh version as well, since the latter is more fully preserved textually. We shall compare Genesis with the Babylonian versions in the hope of seeing more clearly the distinctive features of the theology of Genesis 1–11. We shall ignore differences, such as the size and shape of the ark, which do not seem to be germane to theology.

God and the gods

In Genesis 1 we noted the absence of any rivals to the one creator God. There were no theogonies—stories relating intercourse between gods and goddesses to produce young gods. Indeed, there were no goddesses. In Genesis 1 the sun and moon were called the greater and lesser lights, lest people thought the sun and the moon were gods. The same contrast appears in the flood story. The Babylonian version mentions many gods, often at odds with each other, whereas the Genesis account has just one

---

8. See above, p. 23.

God in total control of events. The character of the gods is quite different in both accounts too. The Babylonian gods send the flood, but when it occurs they are unable to stop it. Instead, they cower like dogs and they retreat to heaven, while the goddesses Ishtar and Belet-ili weep and lament that they agreed to the flood being released. After the flood has ended and all have emerged from the ark, Enlil—one of the top gods—arrived and was surprised to discover some humans had survived. Filled with anger, he said, "What sort of life survived? No man should have lived through the destruction"[9] (Gilgamesh 11.174–75). So, not only are the Babylonian gods deficient in power, they also do not know all that goes on.

Genesis presents a completely different picture of affairs. The one God both knows what is happening in the flood and also is in absolute control of it. The turning point in the narrative is: "But God remembered Noah and all the beasts and all the livestock that were with him in the ark. And God made a wind blow over the earth, and the waters subsided" (Gen 8:1). This simple comment says it all: the God of Genesis is both omnipotent and omniscient. He is not dependent on man as the Babylonian gods are. According to the Atrahasis epic, mankind was created to supply the gods with food by the offering of sacrifice. But destroying the human race in the flood cut off the gods' food supply, so after fourteen days of the flood the gods were hungry! And when Atrahasis (alias Utnapishtim) offered sacrifices

> The gods smelt the pleasant fragrance
> The gods like flies gathered over the sacrifice[10]
> (Gilgamesh 11.160–62)

In Genesis though, it is God who supplies man with food (1:29–30; 9:3–4), not vice versa. Noah's sacrifices appeased God's anger at man's sinful heart, they did not keep God alive!

The divine motivation for the flood is also quite different in the two traditions. According to the Atrahasis epic, the flood was sent to reduce the human population. Too many human beings on earth disturbed the repose of the gods in heaven, so they sent a plague to destroy mankind, and, when that failed, they sent a drought and finally the flood. Genesis is quite clear that it is not overpopulation that prompted God to send a flood, but the evil of the human heart, particularly manifest in violence (6:5, 11, 13). The God of Genesis is concerned to curb human sin, not human fertility.

9. Dalley, *Myths of Mesopotamia*, 115.
10. Ibid., 114.

Rethinking Genesis 6–9

This is underlined by the conclusion to the flood story in Atrahasis. The broken text probably refers to the gods' decision "to institute death as the normal end to human life."[11] They also attempted to limit human fertility by making some women childless and others to suffer from stillbirths or their children to die in infancy. This is quite different from Genesis' pro-life stance. Three times after the flood the creation command to be fruitful and multiply is reiterated (Gen 1:22, 28; 8:17; 9:1, 7). In this way, Genesis retells the ancient story of the flood and paints a completely fresh picture of the nature of God and his expectations of the human race.

The Flood Hero

Further insight into divine ideals for mankind can be derived from the different portrayals of the flood hero in the two traditions. In the Gilgamesh epic it is the flood hero who tells the story, "I did this and I did that." It is an account that essentially glorifies Utnapishtim/Atrahasis. Whereas in Genesis, Noah does not speak, he is just the main human actor in the story. But as we shall see, he is depicted not as heroic, but as obedient.

Utnapishtim/Atrahasis was warned about the flood by the god Ea, the god of wisdom and magic. Ea was one of the top gods, but he disagreed with the decision of the other gods to destroy mankind, so he tipped off his devotee Utnapishtim. On receipt of this advice Utnapishtim reacted very energetically. He mobilized an army of ark builders, who built a huge cube-shaped boat in a few weeks. He supplied them liberally with food and drink

> I gave the workmen ale and beer to drink
> Oil and wine as if they were river water.[12]
> (Gilgamesh 11.72–73)

The launch, he said, was very difficult, but he managed it using rollers. Then he loaded his ark

> I loaded her with everything there was
> Loaded her with all the silver,
> Loaded her with all the gold
> Loaded her with all the seed of living things all of them.

---

11. Ibid., 8.
12. Ibid., 111.

> I put on board the boat all my kith and kin.[13]
>
> (Gilgamesh 11.80–84)

He also loaded it with animals. When the storm began he "went aboard the boat and closed the door"[14] (Gilgamesh 11.93).

After a description of the flood and its destructive power, Utnapishtim resumes his egocentric account:

> I opened a porthole and light fell on my cheek . . .
> When the seventh day arrived
> I put out and released a dove . . . .
> Then I put everything out to the four winds
> And I made a sacrifice.[15]
>
> (Gilgamesh 11.136–56)

The hungry gods greatly appreciated this sacrifice, gathering like flies over it. In this way, Utnapishtim hypes his own achievements and portrays himself as a great hero.

The portrait of Noah painted by Genesis is quite different. We have already noted that it is a third-person description of events, not boastful autobiography. The narrative does not stress the magnitude of Noah's achievements, but rather his complete obedience to God's instructions. A long explanation of how and why he should build the ark is concluded with: "Noah did this; he did all that God commanded him" (Gen 6:22). Similarly, the detailed instruction about entering the ark concludes: "And Noah did all that the LORD had commanded him" (Gen 7:5). The description of the entry into the ark ends with: "And those that entered, male and female of all flesh, went in as God had commanded him. And the LORD shut him in" (Gen 7:16). Whereas Utnapishtim closed the door of the ark himself, *God* shut Noah in.

Noah is not simply described as righteous and blameless in his generation, but his righteousness is shown in action: he does things because God tells him to and, as we noted earlier, he copies God in observing the Sabbath. And Genesis implies that it was for his righteousness that he found favor in God's sight and therefore was saved. It was not, as in Utnapishtim's case, just a matter of good luck that he was advised to build an ark to escape

---

13. Ibid., 111–12.
14. Ibid., 112.
15. Ibid., 113–14.

the deluge. It was an act of divine grace prompted by his walk with God. As the putative father of the whole human race (all other branches of mankind having perished in the flood), Noah stands as an example for all his descendants to follow.

Thus, the Genesis flood story may be seen as both an indirect commentary on Genesis 1–4 and a more explicit refutation of Mesopotamian versions of the flood story. That is not to say the author of Genesis knew the text of the story either in its Atrahasis or Gilgamesh form. Rather, they were part of the cognitive environment, part of the cultural inheritance of those who lived in the ancient orient, just as most modern Westerners are very familiar with the theory of evolution without ever having read the *Origin of Species*.

Certainly an ancient oriental brought up on these ancient oriental traditions would be astonished by Genesis' version. We can imagine him reacting to the biblical tale: "What, only one God, not a tribe of gods and goddesses? And so almighty, separating the water from the land merely by a word or sending the wind! He supplies mankind with food: he does not expect humans to feed him!" The gods of the epics are capricious in handling humans, but the God of Genesis is stern. He expels Adam and Eve from the Garden for merely one small act of disobedience, and could have destroyed the whole human race for their addiction to violence. Whereas most ancients were optimistic about the development of culture, the Genesis flood account emphasizes man's intrinsic sinfulness, which leads inevitably to degeneration. Its hope lies in a God who saved Noah because of Noah's righteousness and promised to spare the human race in future on the ground of that righteous man's sacrifices.

4

Rethinking Genesis 5–11
Creation in Need of Redemption

Introduction

So far we have attempted to discover the nature of the narratives in Genesis 1–9. We have argued that the opening chapter summing up creation in six days of divine activity provides readers of Scripture with the theological spectacles to read the rest of Genesis, if not the whole Bible, with the right presuppositions. It discloses the fundamental character of God, a God who is one, almighty, and concerned for human welfare. In its central beliefs Genesis 1 presents a challenge to the theology of its contemporaries and ours.[1]

The ideas of the opening chapter are filled out, expanded, and clarified in the subsequent chapters. Chapter 2 again discloses the sovereign power of God and his concern for man's welfare by the creation of the Garden of Eden, a centre of abundant life and fertility. As the cosmic mountain, Eden was designed to be a place of unimpeded fellowship between God and man, a place where man and beast coexisted peacefully, a place where man and wife lived in harmonious intimacy. Sadly all these ideals were shattered by Adam and Eve disobeying the one rule given by God for life in the garden. The curses on all these relationships (alienation from God, chauvinism in marriage, and hostility between man and the animal, Gen 3:14–19)

---

1. For a helpful overview of the polemical thrust of Genesis, see Currid, *Against the Gods*.

describe the present human condition, making it clear that Adam's transgression was not just paradigmatic describing what happens when anyone sins, but protohistorical. The human race cannot recover the innocence of the Garden.

Indeed, Genesis portrays a situation that becomes ever darker as the world is engulfed in violence. The consequence is a universal flood to exterminate degenerate humanity and start again with the blameless Noah. So the work of creation is systematically undone, taking much longer than a mere week, and then a new creation is begun with Noah as the new Adam, father of the entire human race. But there are warning signs that the situation is not as rosy as it was in Eden. After the flood, the human heart is still prone to evil and violence is still a problem. This is shown by the final episode, where Noah disgraces himself and Ham assaults him. Having reached 9:27 we must conclude that sin is both chronic and endemic in the human heart. Yet the life of Noah does not leave us without hope. Noah found favor in the eyes of the LORD, because he was righteous and blameless in his generation (6:8–9). Even more hopeful was the LORD's reaction to Noah's sacrifices: "And when the LORD smelled the pleasing aroma, the LORD said in his heart, 'I will never again strike down every living creature as I have done. While the earth remains, seedtime and harvest, cold and heat, summer and winter, day and night, shall not cease'" (Gen 8:21–22).

In this chapter we shall explore further how these two themes of human sin and divine grace are worked out further in the genealogies, the sons of God episode, and the tower of Babel story, and what further light they shed on the nature of these chapters.

The Genealogies in Genesis 5 and 11

We begin by looking at the genealogies and their relationship to the flood story. There are two full genealogies in the opening chapters. The first (Gen 5:1–32) tracks the descendants of Adam through Seth to Noah in ten generations. The second (Gen 11:10–27) does the same for the descendants of Shem to Abram. This takes nine generations, or ten, if one starts with Noah (cf. 9:18; 10:1).[2] Each rung of the genealogies is similar to 5:6–7:

---

2. There is also a short genealogy of the descendants of Cain in 4:17–24 and of Seth in 4:25–26. There is also the genealogy-like Table of Nations in 10:1–32.

> When Seth had lived 105 years, he fathered Enosh.
> Seth lived after he fathered Enosh 807 years and had other sons and daughters.
> Thus, all the days of Seth were 912 years, and he died.

To generalize:

> When A had lived x years, he fathered B.
> A lived after he fathered B y years and had other sons and daughters.
> Thus, all the days of A were x + y years, and he died.

All the items in the first genealogy take this form, but in the second, the final clause is omitted. Thus the formula runs:

> When A had lived x years, he fathered B.
> A lived after he fathered B y years and had other sons and daughters.

Note however that the formula about Noah is split in two: 5:32 is the first part of the formula slightly modified[3]: "After Noah was 500 years old, Noah fathered Shem, Ham, and Japheth." The end of the formula is found in 9:29: "All the days of Noah were 950 years, and he died." In other words, the flood story has been inserted into the genealogy, or perhaps more precisely, attached to the end of the genealogy. The first genealogy makes the antediluvians live improbably long, an issue to which we shall return later, but the use of a genealogy to link Adam to Noah, and then a second genealogy to link Noah to Abram is another example of what Jacobsen term mytho-historical thought, or what I preferred to call protohistory. "This arrangement along a line of time as cause and effect is striking, for it is very much the way a historian arranges his data."[4] The genealogical links suggest that the named figures that precede Abram in these genealogies are just as real as Abraham himself. Or we can approach it from the other end and see Adam's descendants as reproducing his character as well as his physique. Genesis 5:3 suggests this: "when Adam had lived 130 years, he fathered a son in his own likeness, after his image, and named him Seth." Thus, Seth bears the likeness and image of his father.[5] And we are to understand that this similarity continues down the genealogy.

---

3. The variant arises from two very similar letters *he* and *heth*.
4. Jacobsen "Eridu Genesis," 140.
5. On the terms "image" and "likeness," see Wenham, *Genesis 1–15*, 29–32.

Mesopotamian Parallels

In previous chapters we have noted literary parallels to the biblical text, especially the Epic of Atrahasis and the Sumerian Flood Story. Though the ideology of these Mesopotamian tales is very different from Genesis, their plot and narrative structure are sometimes very close, especially in the Gilgamesh epic version of the flood story. There are also close structural parallels to the arrangement of the genealogies in Genesis. These are split in two by the flood story. The first list of antediluvian patriarchs consists of ten generations from Adam to Noah, often living nearly a thousand years. The second list of postdiluvians again consists of ten generations, from Noah to Abram, but only living about 200 years each. This pattern resembles that of the Sumerian King List, which also divides protohistory into two eras, before and after the flood.

Furthermore, those kings who reigned before the flood reigned much longer than those who reigned after the flood. Before the flood, eight, nine, or ten kings (the number depends which text is followed) reigned for a total of 241,000 years, with one alone reaching 36,000 years. Then, says the King List, "the flood swept over the earth." But after the flood, when kingship was again lowered from heaven, the first king of Kish lived a mere 1,200 years, and his successors were equally short-lived. One may well wonder whether the ancients took these numbers literally or whether they were trying to encapsulate some other truth in these amazing figures. Again Jacobsen has drawn attention to these texts' evident interest in chronology, which sets them apart from most myths and folktales "that . . . are not concerned with time at all."[6] He suggests that the Sumerian Flood Story borrowed this structure from the King List, and it would seem that Genesis is working with a similar tradition, but what its *Tendenz* in refashioning this model is not so clear. The lower ages of Genesis have the effect of bringing these people closer to the era of the writer and so less lost in the mists of time. But it may be that there is a completely different sort of explanation that so far has eluded scholars.

---

6. Jacobsen, "Eridu Genesis," 141.

Long Lives: Some Suggestions

The ages of the people recorded in the genealogies present two major problems. First, these patriarchs age very slowly: not only do many nearly reach a thousand before they die, but none of them have children till they are at least sixty-five, and Noah is 500 before he fathers Shem, Ham, and Japhet. The second is more technical: the ordinary Hebrew Masoretic Text, the rival Samaritan text of the Pentateuch, and the Greek translation, the Septuagint, all have different ages for these patriarchs. This is a perplexing text-critical conundrum, which has no obvious solution.[7] We shall therefore just focus on the Masoretic Text[8] and review some of the suggested explanations of the vast ages.

Short years

It is often suggested that the years in Genesis 5 were much shorter than ours: that perhaps one Genesis year equaled one lunar month. This would make the lengths of the patriarchs' lives manageable, but it would make most of the patriarchs too young when they fathered their first child. It is also belied by the chronology of the flood story, which clearly has at least 360 days in a year.

Abbreviated genealogy

Another suggestion is that the genealogies are incomplete, that generations have been omitted, or that each name represents an era when a particular clan flourished. This could be the case in oral genealogies passed on by word of mouth from one generation to another. However, it does not appear that Genesis 5 can be understood this way. At the beginning of the genealogy it is quite clear that Adam is understood to be the literal father of Seth, while at the other end, Noah is clearly the literal father of his three sons, Shem, Ham, and Japhet. Lamech's prayer at the birth of his son Noah also implies there is no generation omitted (Gen 5:29). With these clear indications of sequence it would be special pleading to postulate large gaps elsewhere in the genealogy.

---

7. For further discussion, see Wenham, *Genesis 1–15*, 130–33.
8. The standard Hebrew text, which forms the basis for modern translations.

Mathematical game

A third possibility depends on Mesopotamian mathematics. The Babylonians used a sexagesimal counting system (using the base 60 as opposed to a binary or decimal system, which we use). In support of this suggestion, it has been noted that many of the ages of these patriarchs can easily be generated by factors of 60. Thus Adam's age when Cain was born was 130. This equals $2 \times 60 + 10$. His age at death was $930 = 30^2 + 30$. This is very ingenious, but it is not obvious why they should want to create the ages this way.

Astronomical periods

Babylonian astronomy has also been invoked to explain the ages of the patriarchs at their death. Enoch lived 365 years, the number of days in a solar year. Other ages at death could relate to synodic periods of the planets, that is, to the number of days it takes for a planet to return to its initial position in the sky. Thus Lamech's 777 years can be arrived at by adding the synodic period of Jupiter to that of Saturn, and Yared's 962 by adding the periods of Venus and Saturn. This is even more ingenious than the mathematical explanation, but again there is no obvious reason for producing ages this way.

Theological Implications

To date then no one has come up with a convincing explanation of these numbers. They may well symbolize some truth, but so far no one has cracked the code. If they are symbolic, it is not clear what they symbolize. If they are literal, we are left with the historical problems we started with. We can, though, suggest that these genealogies reinforce some of the theological ideas expressed elsewhere in Genesis 1–11. The first genealogy in Genesis sums up the history of the first creation of the world before the flood. Though short in literary terms, within the time frame of Genesis it covers the longest period in world history. It links Noah to Adam, thereby making Noah a second Adam figure. It also shows mankind fulfilling the command to be fruitful and multiply. It affirms the unity of the human race, for all are descended from Adam, and it underlines that all humans bear the image of God and are responsible for managing creation. There could again be a touch of anti-Mesopotamian polemic in the ages of the antediluvians.

Ancient cultures held that originally humans lived much longer than they did later. Genesis could be scaling down this belief, by showing that even in the furthest past no one reached a thousand years, which is but a day in God's sight (Ps 90:4).

Genesis 6:1–8. A Surprising Coda

Genesis, as already noted, consists of an introductory overture (1:1—2:3) and ten sections, each headed by the formula "This is the history of . . ."/"These are the generations of . . . ." One of these formulae is found in 5:1 and heads the genealogy, but the next is not found till 6:9, "These are the generations of Noah." This implies that 6:1–8 belongs with what precedes it, i.e., the genealogy (Gen 5:1–32). We have already noted that 6:5–8, announcing the flood, is a trailer for the main story in 6:9—9:29. But what is its relationship to 6:1–4, the divine-human marriages, and how does the latter relate to the genealogy in chapter 5? The problem is exacerbated by the difficulty in comprehending what is being described in 6:1–4. I shall therefore begin by reviewing suggested interpretations of these verses, before trying to relate them to their context and their contribution to the message of Genesis 1–11.

Here is the ESV translation of 6:1–4:

> When man began to multiply on the face of the land and daughters were born to them, the sons of God saw that the daughters of man were attractive. And they took as their wives any they chose. Then the LORD said, "My Spirit shall not abide in man forever, for he is flesh: his days shall be 120 years." The Nephilim were on the earth in those days, and also afterward, when the sons of God came in to the daughters of man and they bore children to them. These were the mighty men who were of old, the men of renown.

This passage presents numerous exegetical problems. Who are the sons of God and the daughters of man? Who are the mighty men of old and are they the Nephilim? Why will God's spirit not abide in man forever? What does the 120-year time limit apply to?

Who are the Sons of God?

The sons of God are kings

Three main solutions have been offered to the identity of the sons of God. From the mid-second century AD most Jews have held that the sons of God were kings. The king is called the son of God in 2 Samuel 7:14 and Psalm 2:7, for example. Proponents of this view claim that judges are termed "sons of God" in Psalm 82. On this view, kings or other rulers are abusing their powers to grab pretty girls and enroll them in their polygamous harems. This cruel behavior aroused God's anger, prompting him to limit human life to 120 years.

The sons of God are Sethites

The second view is the Sethite interpretation. This holds that the godly Sethites are the sons of God, and the daughters of man are the descendants of Cain. Genesis presents two genealogies from Adam, the first via Cain (4:17–24) and the second via Seth (5:1–32). It is argued that the Sethite line is the elect line leading via righteous Noah to the chosen race descended from Abraham and Jacob. And the nation of Israel was called God's son (Exod 4:22; Deut 14:1). The Israelites were strictly forbidden to marry outsiders. Here we have that principle flouted by the Sethites. Though this makes sense of the sons of God, it is hard to see why the Cainites should be called the daughters of man; surely this would be a suitable description of a girl of any race?

The sons of God are spirits

The oldest[9] and also the most favored modern interpretation is that the sons of God are supernatural beings inferior to God in ability and power. In modern parlance they would be termed spirits, angels, or demons, depending on their character. Polytheists might simply term them gods, as do some of the psalms (Ps 82:1; 96:4–5; 97:7). The relationship between these so-called gods and the one true God is declared in Psalm 95:3, "For the LORD is a great God, and a great King above all gods." The Old Testament also terms these beings "sons of the gods." The book of Job pictures them attending the

---

9. For further discussion see Wenham, *Genesis 1–15*, 139.

heavenly committee that God chairs (Job 1:6–12; 2:1–7). "Now there was a day when the sons of God came to present themselves before the LORD, and Satan also came among them" (Job 1:6). There follows quite a long discussion between the LORD and the Satan. This understanding of the sons of God also seems to be assumed in the New Testament. "For if God did not spare angels when they sinned, but cast them into hell and committed them to chains of gloomy darkness to be kept until the judgment..." (2 Pet 2:4. Cf. Jude 6). Second Peter seems to be alluding to the interpretation of Genesis 6:1–4 found in *1 Enoch* 6:1—7:6 (a pre-Christian Jewish work), which clearly understands the sons of God to be a kind of angelic being.

To modern readers the idea that spirit beings should have sexual intercourse with humans is hard to swallow, but ancients believed certain heroes were indeed god-human hybrids. Gilgamesh, for example, had a human father and a goddess as his mother. So did Aeneas, while Helen of Troy had Zeus for her father and Leda, a woman, for her mother.[10] Verse 4 states that the Nephilim (cf. Num 13:33) were the offspring of such unions. This tradition about divine-human intercourse may well be the background thinking, but it is only part of the problem.

The next query is: why should humans be blamed for an act initiated by these so-called gods? Perhaps one clue is in the language, which seems to echo Genesis 3:6 "the woman *saw* . . . *good* for food . . . *took* the fruit." Compare that with 6:1–2, in which "the sons of God *saw* that the daughters of man were attractive [lit. good]. And they *took* as their wives any they chose." In both cases we read that the sinners *saw* that X (the fruit, the daughters of men) was *good* and *took* it. In other words, this is a replay of the fall. These echoes underline the gravity of the sin, but they do not explain why humans should be blamed for the gods' behavior.

It may be that the social conventions of ancient marriage clarify the issue. Though the sons of god are sometimes understood to be forcing girls into marriage, there is nothing in the language to require such a reading. The terms used suit a perfectly ordered marriage. In the ancient orient marriage was essentially an arrangement linking two families, an arrangement negotiated chiefly by the males, the groom's father and the bride's father. The latter would have to give his consent to the marriage of his daughter by agreeing the bride price with the groom's family. In this light it is evident that the human party was responsible for consenting to the union, just as Adam was responsible for accepting his wife's invitation to eat the

---

10. Day, *Creation to Babel*, 95.

forbidden fruit in Eden. This episode thus replays some of the essential features of the fall in Genesis 3.

Genesis 3 concludes with God expelling Adam and Eve from the garden, "lest he reach out his hand and take also of the tree of life and eat, and live forever" (3:22). On that occasion God punished sin by depriving mankind of immortality, though many still lived a very long time. This time he punishes sin by limiting human life to 120 years. "Then the LORD said, 'My Spirit shall not abide in man forever, for he is flesh: his days shall be 120 years'" (Gen 6:3).

But the shortened lifespan does not really deal with the problem of inveterate sin, and there follows one of the most damning assessments of human sinfulness in the whole Bible: "The LORD saw that the wickedness of man was great in the earth, and that every intention of the thoughts of his heart was only evil continually. And the LORD regretted that he had made man on the earth, and it grieved him to his heart" (Gen 6:5–6).

A general condemnation of human behavior—"the wickedness of man was great in the earth"—is followed by a very severe analysis of the root problem. Verse 6 could be more literally translated "every idea of the plans of his heart was nothing but evil all the time." The heart is the centre of man's personality, combining the functions we ascribe to the mind and the will, as well as the emotions. It is what drives someone. It is what makes a person what he is. It creates ideas and formulates plans, but according to Genesis 6:5 these thoughts and feelings are all marred by sin. Note the emphasis on the ubiquity of corruption of the will "*every* idea nothing but evil *all the time.*" This verse asserts that every thought is essentially evil from its beginning. Few texts are so explicit and all-embracing in their analysis of human depravity. But that sin often has its origin in the thought world is an accepted axiom of biblical ethics (e.g., Pss 14:1–3; 51:1–10; Jer 13:23).

It is the extent and depth of human sin that prompts the extreme reaction of God: "And the LORD regretted that he had made man on the earth, and it grieved him to his heart" (Gen 6:6). When God regrets or repents in response to human behavior, he acts differently. But this is no ordinary change of heart: "it *grieved* him to his heart." Grief is an under-translation. God was *bitterly indignant*, like Dinah's brothers were when they heard of her rape, like Jonathan was when he learned of his father's plan to kill David, like David after he heard of Absalom's death, like a deserted wife (Gen 34:7; 1 Sam 20:34; 2 Sam 19:2; Isa 54:6). In other words, this grieving was a powerful and bitter regret. So God plans to wipe out mankind. In this way these short verses not only link back to the earlier stories, reinforcing the significance of the fall, but they act as a trailer to the next great block of material, the flood narrative, introduced by "These are the generations of Noah." "So the LORD said, 'I will blot out man whom I have created from the face of the land, man and animals and creeping things and birds of the heavens, for I am sorry that I have made them'" (Gen 6:7).

Here Genesis reasserts the enormous danger of sin. It is not only self-destructive, it is hateful to God and attracts his judgment of death. But in this desperately dark situation there is one glimmer of hope: "Noah found favor in the eyes of the LORD" (Gen 6:8).

This is unpacked in the detailed account of the flood and its aftermath. Noah, the second Adam, head of the only family to survive the deluge shows his strict adherence to the law by obeying God's commands to build the ark and by observing the Sabbath. This is a promising start for the new creation, but Noah's drunkenness and his son's disrespect shows that the new order will not be sinless. Mankind does survive and, as the Table of Nation shows in chapter 10, it fulfilled the mandate to be fruitful and fill the earth. But as one final tale in Genesis 11 reminds us, this spread of humanity is not without its downside. The Tower of Babel is a monument to human folly and pride.

The Tower of Babel

Like the surprising coda in Genesis 6:1–8, the story of the Tower of Babel (Gen 11:1–9) is tacked on to a long, essentially genealogical, section (Gen 10:1–32), and, like that earlier coda, it does not seem to have much to do with the main section, in this case the Table of Nations. But like that coda, it reaffirms God's readiness to judge rebellious mankind. The promise not to destroy the world in another flood does not mean mankind can get away with whatever it likes. Bringing to a close the protohistory, this episode underscores the message of humanity's inveterate sinfulness and the need for divine intervention if mankind is to be redeemed: the call of Abraham which follows in chapter 12 begins the story of that redemption.

The structure of the narrative

The Tower of Babel story is short compared with other narratives in Genesis 1–11, but it is, like earlier stories, well structured and best read against the background of Mesopotamian mythology. Like the flood story the Tower of Babel narrative is arranged as a palistrophe:

A The whole earth had one language (v. 1)
  B There (v. 2)
    C one another (v. 3)
      D Come, let us make bricks
        E let us build ourselves
          F a city and a tower (v. 4)
            G the LORD came down (v. 5)
          F' to see the city and the tower
        E' which the children of man had built
      D' Come, let us go down and . . . confuse their language (v. 7)
    C' one another's speech
  B' from there (v. 8)
A' the language of the whole earth (v. 9)

This palistrophe is not as clear-cut as that in the flood story, but it does serve a dramatic purpose. The turning point in this story is like that in the flood. There the turning point was "But God remembered Noah" (Gen 8:1). Here the turning point is "The LORD came down to see the city and the tower" (Gen 11:5). God's intervention again thwarts man's plans. Humans thought they were building a tower whose top would be in the heavens. But so far from reaching heaven were their efforts that God had to come down and have a look: in heaven he could hardly see this so-called skyscraper!

The second half of the palistrophe accentuates the sarcastic humor of this story by making God echo in deed and word the men of Babel's words and acts. They say, "Come, let us make bricks." God says, "Come, let us go down and confuse their language." They want to build a city and tower, "lest we be dispersed over the face of the whole earth." But that is exactly what God did: "The LORD dispersed them from there over the face of the whole earth" (Gen 11:9).[11] Like the expulsion of Adam and Eve from the garden, the dispersal of the nations is a preemptive strike lest the sinners trespass

---

11. In the Hebrew, God mocks the tower-builders even more obviously: "Let us make bricks" (*nilběnāh*) becomes "Let us confuse" (*nābělāh*), which also sounds like "folly" (*něbālāh*).

even further on God's domains, by eating from the tree of life in the first case and doing things that should be impossible in the second.

Mesopotamian parallels

As with other stories in early Genesis, scholars have detected possible Mesopotamian parallels that could be alluded to and commented on, but they are not so obvious as the versions of the flood story. The confusion of tongues in Genesis could be commentary on Enmerkar and the Lord of Aratta. This Sumerian epic mentions a golden era in which everyone dwells in peace and speaks the same language, Sumerian. But translators disagree whether this golden age is past or future. Is this text looking back to a time when everyone spoke Sumerian until the god Enki upset the regime? Or is it looking forward to an age of unity among the peoples when all will speak Sumerian? The first interpretation sounds more like Genesis, the second more like Zephaniah 3:9, which looks forward to an age when God will "change the speech of all peoples to a pure speech."

On the first interpretation, Genesis 11 is offering an alternative explanation of the diversity of languages to the Sumerian tale. Whereas the Sumerians ascribed the multitude of languages to a squabble between rival gods, Genesis sees it as a judgment on human pride and arrogance. Here, as in the flood story, Genesis explains the situation in terms of a moral monotheism, not as a product of rivalry between the gods.

On the second interpretation, which sees Sumerian as the future world language, Genesis is making a different point. The Sumerians saw other cultures as evolving positively *towards* a Sumerian utopia. In their eyes, diversity of language was a bad thing because it prevented people worshipping the great god Enlil. As we have seen frequently in Genesis 1–11, the Bible does not share such optimism about the direction of social change. Genesis holds that the confusion of languages is a divine antidote to human arrogance. Whereas Mesopotamia saw the human condition as improving, Genesis sees it as deteriorating. On this view, the Sumerian epic is vaunting the superiority of its civilization.

Whichever view of the Enmerkar epic and its relationship to Genesis 11 is taken, it is clear that Genesis rejects its claim to the superiority of Babylon. Mesopotamian cities had ziggurats, pyramids with a temple on top. Babylon's temple was called Esagila. It was claimed that its foundations were in the underworld and its top reached the heavens. Further, that the

Rethinking Genesis 5–11

great gods—Marduk, Enlil, and Ea—would take their rest in the temple. These claims as we have seen are mocked in Genesis: the building was so far from reaching heaven that God had to come down to even see it.

But with one last comment Genesis finally dismisses Babylon's pretensions: "Therefore its name was called Babel, because there the LORD confused the language of all the earth. And from there the LORD dispersed them over the face of all the earth" (Gen 11:9). To appreciate the force of this put-down, one must realize that in Akkadian *Babil* means "Gate of God." In other words, Babylon—not Ur, Jerusalem, Mecca, or Rome—is the place to meet God. "Nonsense!" says Genesis. In a disrespectful pun on the Hebrew for Babylon (*bābel*), Genesis says that *bābel* means confusion. (*Bābel* means "he confused.") God's comment, "Let us confuse" (*nābēlāh*), also sounds like "folly" *nĕbālāh*. Babylonians think Babel means "Gate of God," but Genesis says it means "confusion" and "folly."

So at last the gloves are off! Throughout Genesis 1–11 we have noted a steady retelling of ancient Near Eastern tales, especially as they are known in Babylonian sources. Instead of polytheism Genesis gives a monotheistic interpretation of world history from creation to the flood. Instead of gods unable to control fully the forces of nature, Genesis tells of one almighty God who has total sovereignty over all other powers. Instead of seeing man as an afterthought made for the convenience and comfort of the gods, Genesis says the world was created for man's benefit, and far from man supplying the gods with food, God cares for man. Instead of catastrophes befalling the human race because of the caprice of the gods, Genesis says mankind has brought divine judgment on itself through its transgression of divine law and its addiction to violence. The Babylonians may think life is improving, but Genesis says the dispersal of the human race and its diversity of languages is proof that God acts against all those who delude themselves that they are in ultimate control. The hope for the human race lies in a new divine initiative of grace. From Ur, a town south of Babylon, God will call Abraham, to head a new humanity that will succeed where Adam, Noah, and Babylon failed.

5

Epilogue
The Hope of New Creation

Introduction

WE HAVE NOW REACHED the end of my rethinking of Genesis 1–11. At the start I mentioned the danger of letting our interpretation of Genesis be too influenced by our assumptions. I have tried to achieve a measure of objectivity, or at least some sensitivity to the author's intention, by setting Genesis 1–11 within the context of ancient oriental beliefs about primeval times. I have concentrated on Mesopotamian texts because they furnish the closest parallels to the Bible. An ancient Iraqi encountering Genesis' version of his traditions would not be struck by its similarity to the tales he was brought up with, but by the differences. And so I have focused on bringing out the implications of these differences for ancient readers.

It is these differences that we need to pay close attention to, if we are to let the texts speak for themselves. But inevitably Christian readers will want to ask how the theology and ethics of Genesis 1–11 fit with New Testament ideas. And both religious and secular readers are interested in comparing biblical ideas about cosmology and origins with modern scientific theories. To do either task properly would be a huge undertaking, and all I can offer are a few superficial observations in the hope that a few crumbs are better than no bread.

So I shall risk the ire of the knowledgeable and attempt to answer two questions. First, how do the ideas of Genesis 1–11 fit with other expressions of biblical theology, especially the New Testament? And second, how does the biblical theology of origins look in the light of modern science-based theories of origins?

Genesis 1–11 and Biblical Theology

Divine Unity and Sovereignty

Fundamental to Genesis 1 is the unity of God. This is the first big contrast with the competing religions of the ancient world. God's unity and uniqueness run through Scripture. "Hear, O Israel, the LORD Our God, the LORD is one" (Deut 6:4) is endorsed by Jesus (Mark 12:29). The first commandment draws out the implication "You shall have no other gods before me." Yet Israel disobeys this fundamental commandment. Repeatedly Israel sins by worshipping other gods, setting up shrines in their honor and offering sacrifice to them. This behavior, according to Israel's prophets and historians, prompted the exile.

The unity of God is taken for granted by the New Testament. Jesus cites the Shema (Mark 12:29–30). St. Paul is equally dogmatic: "yet for us there is one God, the Father, from whom are all things and for whom we exist, and one Lord, Jesus Christ, through whom are all things and through whom we exist" (1 Cor 8:6); "he . . . is the blessed and only Sovereign, the King of kings and Lord of lords" (1 Tim 6:15).

A corollary of God's unity and uniqueness is his sovereignty, another fundamental of biblical theology. It is first disclosed in the commands that bring the cosmos into being, "Let there be light," "Let the dry land appear." God's control is exhibited in the flood story too. When God remembers Noah, he puts the process of de-creation into reverse and the new creation begins. Psalms and prophets assert divine sovereignty too. Psalm 2 pictures God laughing at those who think they can flout divine authority, while Psalms 93–100 repeatedly declare "The LORD reigns!" The Gospels tell us that Jesus is the one whom winds and waves obey (Matt 8:27). He declares that not a sparrow falls to the ground without the Father knowing it (Matt 10:29). The book of Revelation proclaims, "the Lord God omnipotent reigneth" (19:6 AV).

Human Dignity and Sin

Contemplating God's handiwork in creation Psalm 8:4 asks:

> What is man that you are mindful of him,
> and the son of man that you care for him?

Yet both the psalm and Genesis agree that man is indeed special, because he alone of all created beings is made in the image of God. This makes him God's representative on earth, charged with managing it on God's behalf. In other cultures kings were seen as God's representatives, but Genesis 1:27 makes *every* human being, male and female, God's image bearer. This idea—that humans are in that image—is central to New Testament soteriology, because Christ is the image of the invisible God (Col 1:15) and Christians are those being transformed into that image (Rom 8:29; cf. 1 Cor 15:49).

This transformation is required because, as Genesis and subsequent biblical writers affirm, the heart of man is desperately corrupt (e.g., Jer 17:9). Genesis 6:5 speaks of every intention of the human heart being only evil continually. That is why the flood was sent (Gen 6:6–7). Psalmists concur:

> They have all turned aside; together they have become corrupt;
>> there is none who does good,
>> not even one.
>
> (Ps 14:3)

> Enter not into judgment with your servant,
>> for no one living is righteous before you.
>
> (Ps 143:2)

David in Psalm 51:5 states that his sinful nature began with his conception;

> Behold, I was brought forth in iniquity,
> and in sin did my mother conceive me.

Jeremiah thinks that sin is as intrinsic to man as spots are to a leopard (Jer 13:23). Jesus shares this gloomy assessment of the human heart when he says: "For from within, out of the heart of man, come evil thoughts, sexual immorality, theft, murder, adultery, coveting, wickedness, deceit, sensuality, envy, slander, pride, foolishness" (Mark 7:21–22).

Epilogue

In Romans 3 Paul cites a string of verses from the Psalter to establish the same point.

> It is written:
> "None is righteous, no, not one;
>> no one understands;
>> no one seeks for God.
> All have turned aside; together they have become worthless;
>> no one does good,
>> not even one."
> "Their throat is an open grave;
>> they use their tongues to deceive."
> "The venom of asps is under their lips."
>> "Their mouth is full of curses and bitterness."
> "Their feet are swift to shed blood;
>> in their paths are ruin and misery,
> and the way of peace they have not known."
>> "There is no fear of God before their eyes."
> (Rom 3:10–18)

Yet both testaments declare and show God's concern for man despite his sin. At the height of the flood God remembers Noah. He mitigates Cain's punishment. And though God's analysis of the human heart in 8:21 resembles that in 6:5 Noah's burnt offerings lead to God declaring that he will never again destroy the earth in a flood. Here we have foreshadowed the sacrifice of Christ and its saving efficacy. One could say Noah, the first Second Adam, by his sacrifices secured the salvation of the world from destruction in another flood. Jesus, the second Second Adam, made atonement for the sins of the whole world through his own death the perfect sacrifice.

Divine Dwelling and Other Themes

God's rest on the seventh day is the goal of his creative work. The Sabbath, like the Garden of Eden, was designed to enable God to dwell with man. This too is the goal that the New Testament dreams of. For a few years God was present on earth in the person of Jesus, the Incarnate Word, and today divine presence is partially realized by the indwelling of the Spirit in the believer. But it remains a goal that will be fully realized only in the new heaven and earth. "And I heard a loud voice from the throne saying, 'Behold, the dwelling place of God is with man. He will dwell with them, and they will be his people, and God himself will be with them as their God'" (Rev 21:3).[1]

This does not exhaust the picture. One might cite the way both Jesus and Paul appeal to Genesis 1 and 2 for their understanding of marriage (Matt 19:3–12; Eph 5:31) or Jesus' warnings about judgment (Matt 24:37–39). It would be fruitful to draw out many other points of contact between Genesis 1–11 and the rest of Scripture, but I hope I have given sufficient reason for holding that there is substantial continuity in the theological themes linking the first chapters in the Bible to the last, Genesis 1 to Revelation 22.

Genesis 1–11 and Modern Science

But is this biblical theology in any way compatible with modern science? One might start a response with Genesis 1:3, "'Let there be light,' and there was light." This could be an apt description of the Big Bang, which marked the beginning of the universe. Or one might point to the anthropic principle, which asserts that many of the fundamental constants of the universe (e.g., gravity) seem to be just right for life to survive and man to emerge.[2] The geological record shows that man is the most highly developed of all known living creatures, just as Genesis 1 and the Psalms see his creation as the most wonderful of all God's works.

Such a concordist approach is helpful. So too are the observations of people who point to weak points in the standard evolutionary models of the development of life in its various forms. They remind us of the limitations of scientific theory. The "intelligent design" advocates say these gaps in scientific explanation point to divine intervention. That may well be so, but believers in creation should see God at work, not just in places that scientists cannot explain, but *everywhere*. God's power and wisdom are exhibited throughout the creation, not just in the inexplicable, but in the well-understood phenomena. As a gardener I marvel at the beauty of the flowers and their variety, at the vigor of the weeds, which seem to spring up overnight. As a holidaymaker I am overwhelmed by the extent and power

1. See also Heb 4:1–10.
2. For further discussion, see Holder, *Big Bang, Big God*, 84–115.

Epilogue

of the sea, especially when it is rough. These displays of God's wisdom and power should make us exclaim:

> O LORD, how manifold are your works!
> In wisdom have you made them all;
> the earth is full of your creatures.
> (Ps 104:24)

And the discoveries of modern science are even more amazing. Awe is too weak a term for our response to the theories of cosmology, on the one hand, and the findings of biochemistry, on the other. What must our God be like if he created and sustains this universe. It contains, we are told, 100 billion galaxies, each made up of 100 billion stars, each as powerful as our sun. "Almighty" and "omnipotent" take on a new meaning when we apply them to the Creator of our universe. And then there is the big bang, that event 13.8 million years ago, when all the material that makes up the stars and galaxies suddenly exploded out from an infinitely small and hot point to begin the process of forming our universe. The scientific description of the big bang takes some believing. But again I ask: what must our God be like if he designed and managed the big bang?

At the other end of the scale, the living cell is an amazing testimony to the divine wisdom. An Australian microbiologist gave this description of a cell in language the layman can understand.

> To grasp the reality of life as it has been revealed by molecular biology, we must magnify a cell a thousand million times until it is twenty kilometres in diameter and resembles a giant airship large enough to cover a great city like London or New York. What we would then see would be an object of unparalleled complexity and adaptive design. On the surface of the cell we would see millions of openings, like the port holes of a vast space ship, opening and closing to allow a continual stream of materials to flow in and out. If we were to enter one of these openings we would find ourselves in a world of supreme technology and bewildering complexity. We would see endless highly organized corridors and conduits branching in every direction away from the perimeter of the cell, some leading to the central memory bank in the nucleus and others to assembly plants and processing units. The nucleus itself would be a vast spherical chamber more than a kilometre in diameter, resembling a geodesic dome inside of which we would

see, all neatly stacked together in ordered arrays, the miles of coiled chains of DNA molecules.[3]

Again I ask: what must God be like, if he designed and created the cell?

In reading Genesis 1–11 we repeatedly saw Genesis taking familiar ancient beliefs and stories about origins and giving them a new monotheistic spin. These stories were their equivalent of our modern theories of origins. Doubtless Babylonians believed these tales with as much fervor as modern scientists cling to theirs. But Genesis says that in many respects these old stories give a wrong impression of God and his ways. Dare we say the same about modern cosmological and evolutionary theory? Could we take a leaf out of Genesis' apologetic method?

Atheists say that the developments in the universe in the last 14 billion years have been solely driven by the laws of nature and chance. I do not doubt that the changes down the millennia tracked by astrophysicists, geologists, biologists, and others are in large measure correct, but as Christians we affirm that this not the whole story: God initiated the whole process, drove it, and continues to energize and direct it. It is not just chance. Furthermore, the works of God give us an insight into the character of God. They speak of a God of infinite power and wisdom. As Genesis retold the stories of origin current in the ancient Near East to give a true theological picture of the nature of God, so modern Christians, especially competent scientists, should be retelling contemporary accounts of origins to explain the character of God. This does not mean contradicting the empirical discoveries of cosmologists, geologists, and biochemists, but rather putting their discoveries into a framework that recognizes the work of a purposeful Creator in it all, that our universe is not just the product of freak chance.

One of the most celebrated defenders of atheism in the twentieth century was the philosopher Antony Flew. But in 2004 he announced that he now believed in God. He had been converted, not simply by reviewing the philosophical arguments but by the discoveries of modern science. He writes:

> Why do I believe this, given that I expounded and defended atheism for more than a half century? The short answer is this: this is the world picture, as I see it, that has emerged from modern science. Science spotlights three dimensions of nature that point to God. The first is the fact that nature obeys laws. The second is the

3. Denton, *Evolution*, 328.

dimension of life, of intelligently organized and purpose-driven beings, which arose from matter. The third is the very existence of nature.[4]

When I was a child, I remember seeing Facts of Faith films. They used David-Attenborough-style photography, but the commentary encouraged us to marvel at, say, the bat's echo-sounding system or the migration of birds. What I should like to see is a renewed effort to make people reflect on the wonders of nature and encourage them to ask: what is God like, if he can create and control all this? This will take a huge change of mindset for those brought up to see science as an investigation that has no need of the God hypothesis. But if it could be achieved we shall be able to sing with renewed conviction:

> The heavens declare the glory of God,
>   And the sky above proclaims his handiwork.
> (Ps 19:1)

---

4. Flew, *There is a God*, 88–89.

Bibliography

St. Augustine. *The City of God*. Translated by Marcus Dods. Edinburgh: T. & T. Clark, 1871.
Blenkinsopp, Joseph. *Creation, Un-creation, Re-creation*. London: T. & T. Clark, 2011.
Burnside, Jonathan P. *God, Justice and Society*. New York: Oxford University Press, 2011.
Calvin, John. *A Commentary on Genesis*. Translated by John King. 1847. Reprint. London: Banner of Truth Trust, 1965.
Currid, John D. *Against the Gods: The Polemical Theology of the Old Testament*. Wheaton, IL: Crossway, 2013.
Dalley, Stephanie. *Myths from Mesopotamia: Creation, the Flood, Gilgamesh, and Others*. Rev. ed. Oxford World Classics. Oxford: Oxford University Press, 2000.
Day, John. *From Creation to Babel: Studies in Genesis 1–11*. London: Bloomsbury, 2013.
Delitzsch, Franz. *A New Commentary on Genesis*. 1888. Reprint. Edinburgh: T. & T. Clark, 1978.
Denton, Michael. *Evolution: A Theory in Crisis*. London: Barnett, 1985.
Flew, Antony. *There is a God: How the World's Most Notorious Atheist Changed His Mind*. New York: HarperCollins, 2007.
Gagnon, Robert A. J. *The Bible and Homosexual Practice*. Nashville: Abingdon, 2001.
Gunkel, Hermann. *Creation and Chaos in the Primeval Era and the Eschaton: A Religio-Historical Study of Genesis 1 and Revelation 12*. Translated by K. William Whitney, Jr. Grand Rapids: Eerdmans, 2006. (English translation of *Schöpfung und Chaos in Urzeit und Endzeit*. Göttingen: Vandenhoeck & Ruprecht, 1895).
Hess, Richard S., and David T. Tsumura, eds. *"I Studied Inscriptions from before the Flood": Literary and Linguistic Approaches to Genesis*. Sources for Biblical and Theological Study, Old Testament Series. Winona Lake, IN: Eisenbrauns, 1994.
Holder, Rodney D. *Big Bang, Big God: A Universe Designed for Life?* Oxford: Lion, 2013.
Jacobsen, Thorkild. "The Eridu Genesis." In *"I Studied Inscriptions from before the Flood": Literary and Linguistic Approaches to Genesis*, edited by Richard Hess and David Tsumura, 129–42. Winona Lake, IN: Eisenbrauns, 1994. (Originally published in *Journal of Biblical Literature* 100 (1981) 513–29.)
Jaubert, Annie. *La date de la cène*. Paris: Gabalda, 1957.
Lambert, Wilfred G. "A New Look at the Babylonian Background to Genesis." In *"I Studied Inscriptions from before the Flood": Literary and Linguistic Approaches to Genesis*, edited by Richard Hess and David Tsumura, 96–113. Winona Lake, IN: Eisenbrauns, 1994. (Originally published in *Journal of Theological Studies* 16 (1965) 287–300.)
Lowery, Daniel D. *Toward a Poetics of Genesis 1–11*. Winona Lake, IN: Eisenbrauns, 2013.

Bibliography

Meyers, Carol L. *The Tabernacle Menorah*. Missoula, MT: Scholars, 1976.

Morales, L. Michael *The Tabernacle Pre-figured: Cosmic Mountain Ideology in Genesis and Exodus*. Leuven: Peters, 2012.

Postell, Seth D. *Adam as Israel: Genesis 1-3 as the Introduction to the Torah and Tanakh*. Eugene, OR: Pickwick, 2011.

von Rad, Gerhard. *Genesis: A Commentary*. 2nd ed. London: SCM, 1972.

Walton, John H. *Genesis 1 as Ancient Cosmology*. Winona Lake, IN: Eisenbrauns, 2011.

———. *The Lost World of Genesis 1: Ancient Cosmology and the Origins Debate*. Downers Grove, IL: IVP, 2009.

Weinfeld, Moshe. "Sabbath, Temple and the Enthronement of the LORD." In *Mélanges bibliques et orientaux en l'honneur de M. Henri Cazelles*, edited by A. Caquot and M. Delcor, 501-12. Kevelaer, Germany: Verlag Butzon und Bercker, 1981.

Wenham, Gordon J. "The Coherence of the Flood Narrative." In *"I Studied Inscriptions from before the Flood": Literary and Linguistic Approaches to Genesis*, edited by Richard Hess and David Tsumura, 436-47. Winona Lake, IN: Eisenbrauns, 1994. (Originally published in *Vetus Testamentum* 28 (1978) 336-48.)

———. *Genesis 1-15*. Word Biblical Commentaries 1A. Waco, TX: Word, 1987.

———. "Method in Pentateuchal Source Criticism." *Vetus Testamentum* 41 (1991) 84-109.

Westermann, Claus. *Genesis 1-11: A Commentary*. Translated by John J. Scullion. Minneapolis: Augsburg, 1984.

www.ingramcontent.com/pod-product-compliance
Lightning Source LLC
Chambersburg PA
CBHW022119090426
42743CB00008B/924